GERMAN DOLLS

Identification & Values

Patricia Smith

COLLECTOR BOOKS

A Division of Schroeder Publishing Co., Inc.

The current values in this book should be used only as a guide. They are not intended to set prices, which vary from one section of the country to another. Auction prices as well as dealer prices vary greatly and are affected by condition as well as demand. Neither the Author nor the Publisher assumes responsibility for any losses that might be incurred as a result of consulting this guide.

Cover Doll: Full length view of "King Olav" of Norway. See Kling section. Courtesy Elizabeth Burke.

Additional copies of this book may be ordered from:

COLLECTOR BOOKS
P.O. Box 3009
Paducah, Kentucky 42001

@ $9.95 Add $1.00 for postage and handling.

Copyright: Patricia R. Smith, 1985
ISBN: 0-89145-296-6

This book or any part thereof may not be reproduced without the written consent of the Author and Publisher.

CONTENTS

CREDITS

Thank you to the following for sharing your dolls and helping to get a good cross section of German children for this book.
Photographs by owner unless noted.

Lori Bates
Kitty Best
Shirley Bertrand
Elizabeth Burke, photos by Gunner Burke
Marlowe Cooper
Rosalind Cranor
Pauly Deem, photos by Margaret Mandel
Barbara Earnshaw
Bess Fantl, photos by Penny Pendelbury
Jo Fasnacht, photos by L.B. Gerdes & L.J. Folse
Sally Freeman
O.D. Gregg
Margaret Gunnels, photos by Dwight Smith
Pauline Hoch, photos by McKenna
Diane Hoffman, photos by Margo Kelly
Kimport Dolls, photos by Dwight Smith
Jill Koons
Florence Maine, photos by Wendell Maine
Margaret Mandel
Alice Metherd, photos by Margaret Mandel
Jay Minter, photos by Dwight Smith
Cynthia Orgeron, photos by Venta
Penny Pendlebury, photos by Chuck Pendelbury
Elsie & Marion Reins, photos by Marion Reins
Jimmy & Faye Rodolfos, photos by Faye Rodolfos
Patricia Smith, photos by Dwight Smith
Pat Timmons

DOLLS OF GERMANY

From the early papier mache and into the use of bisque for heads, the German "child-face" was devoid of all emotions and represented the maker's concept of children.

The word "character", by 1910, began to mean realistic. It was not an entirely new concept as attempts had been made before, such as the multi-faced laughing and crying dolls, but what was peculiar to the 20th Century was the determination of German makers to attempt to model dolls after real children.

Kammer and Rinehardt (K star R), with Simon and Halbig making the heads, began in 1909 with model #100 called "Baby", known to collectors as "The Kaiser Baby". The name is incorrect, but collectors will continue to use this term. The doll was made with complete realistic features, and the arms are modeled in different positions, thereby acquiring the name "Kaiser Baby". The Kaiser Wilhelm (who was far from being an infant in 1909) was born with a slight deformity to one hand.

After the introduction of "Baby", Kammer and Rinehardt produced an entire series of character children for the market, from models #101, "pouties" named "Peter" and "Marie", right up through #131 which is a large-eyed googly.

The most common baby by Kammer and Rinehardt to be found is mold #126, and is referred to as a "character" baby. It usually has flirty eyes and also can be found on a toddler body (1927). Some of these #126 babies are more mechanical and may have a clock mechanism inside the head for moving the eyes from side to side. One model has a mechanism within the torso that lowers and raises the arms.

By the mid-1920's, Kammer and Rinehardt dropped most of the character dolls, although #115 was still offered, and by 1927, even baby #100 had ceased to be offered.

Other German dollmakers created character dolls and the leading one was Gebruder Heubach of Lichte in Thuringia, Germany. An entire collection could be built from this one maker of character dolls.

Some early attempts at character babies by J.D. Kestner are highly prized by collectors. These were bisque shoulder heads with dimpled cheeks and open/closed mouths. One was a girl-type with an oddly-shaped kid body with lower arms of composition. Kestner developed many character children that included mold numbers such as 184 and 208, plus the 100 and 200 series of googlies. Kestner's two most collectable characters are the "Hilda" baby and the mold #172 "Gibson Girl".

Character dolls by Armand Marseille are rare, as they generally produced along making the "dolly" face dolls, but some of the more "character" mold numbers by them were: 400, 401, 500 and 701. They did produce a number of different googlies with mold numbers 310, 323,

353, etc. All the googly-eyed dolls were a caricature of the character doll trend. They were amusing, whimsical and very individual.

Simon and Halbig made a great many character heads for other manufacturers and, in relation, not too many that just bear the S & H mark. Some of their own character mold numbers are: 151, 153, 905, 949, 969, 1388, 1488, etc.

One German maker that had an outstanding line of character dolls was Kley and Hahn. The eyes are generally painted, (although glass eyes are found in some) and the modeling was true to life. These mold numbers include 143, 190, 520, 525, 549, 526 523, 531, 546, etc.

Almost all the German makers of dolls tried their hand at the characters, and some were made for the American market, such as American designer George Averill's "Bonnie Baby", Rose O'Neill's "Kewpies" and the Grace Storey Putnum's "Bye-lo" baby.

As doll collecting continues to attract thousands of new enthusiasts, the more advanced collectors move more and more into the realm of the character dolls. The advanced collector has all the "pretty" dolls she wants, and begins to look for the unusual.

HOW TO USE THE PRICE GUIDE

Bisque dolls are gaged mainly by the quality of the head, both in the rarity of the mold and in the fineness of the bisque itself. The painting of the bisque should be flawless with no blotches or white "scuff" marks, nor any pits, pock marks or black dots. The eye holes should be cut out in an even manner with both being near the same size. Many doll's heads were held in an upright position to cut one eye hole, then reversed upside down to cut the other side and sometimes the one eyehole will be "reversed" or enlarged.

Two, three or four dolls of the same mold can appear very different because of the quality of the artist's workmanship. Quality of bisque is actually a personal experience as some collectors do not object to "higher" color, while others prefer almost white bisque. Others may like pale pinkness, but the price of the doll should be reflected in this quality. A doll with "high" coloring (a later doll) such as S.F.B.J., Unis and many made after 1910, should not have as high a price (unless they are character dolls) as ones made earlier with fine bisque.

Doll prices have always been based on the bisque and body conditions, with the bisque being the most important factor. The body must be the correct one--French for a French head and German for a German head. If the head is a shoulder head it should be on a correct style body. For top dollar, the doll should have an original or appropriate body that is old and all in good condition. Minor damage, such as scuffs, a few paint flakes, chipped fingers or toes are minor, and a well repaired old body is much more desirable than a new body. Many of the later German dolls, especially the "character" bisque came on crude "stick" bodies or five-piece poor mache ones. But even if not liked, these have to be acceptable as original to the head. Some bodies actually denote the price of the dolls, such as a lady-type body, jointed toddler bodies, or some of the adorable tiny 8" and under bisque heads on fully jointed (even wrist, elbows and knees) bodies.

The quality of the bisque is of upmost importance in pricing a doll, and it is important that there are no breaks, hairline cracks, cracked or broken shoulder plates, eye chips, any mends or repairs at all, plus the QUALITY of the doll painting should be very, very good to excellent. If any doll is less than perfect the price should be less than for a perfect quality doll.

It is rare to find an old doll that has not been played with, mint and original, so the original clothes play no part in pricing for this book. If a doll has original wig and clothes, and is "mint", then a greater price should be asked for that special doll.

No matter what is said about prices, the collectors set their own prices by what they are willing to pay for a certain doll. Plus they will pay more for dolls they are especially hunting for, or for the fine character dolls. If an individual or dealer places too high a price on a doll, it will most likely go unsold for a long time. If the price is not reduced, the price will gain acceptance through the natural rate of inflation over a period of time.

Popularity of a certain doll moves prices up. For example the "Hilda" baby is so popular that the prices are based on that popularity and demand, and it is fortunate that the QUALITY of 99% of the "Hildas" is excellent, for there are a great many other babies with equal quality, charm, but not the popularity.

ALL BISQUE

Among the all-bisque dolls, the ones with swivel necks are the most desirable because they are rarer, and may be French. Of the swivel neck dolls, a few may have the French loop molded onto the base of the neck. These loops are easily identified as they look like the top of a bell: 🔔

The German swivel heads that are strung without a wooden neck plug have holes at the sides of the neck ⇒▷ ◁ and the head is strung with the arm rubber. These heads will not hold a "turned" position, but will snap back to face the front.

Many of the French-type all-bisque dolls are peg-strung and a few will have painted eyes, but most will have glass eyes and well painted lashes. In the very small sizes, the eyes are usually set and are generally blue with no pupils. As the dolls get larger they are made with pupils and sleep eyes.

French-type legs are much more varied, thinner and more delicate than the German-made all-bisque dolls. They are generally barefooted, although many have vertical as well as circular ribbed stocking in many colors including white, blue, brown, black and yellow. The molded shoes can be high top boots with pointed toes or high buttoned ones with four or more straps. They may have brown, pink, blue or black one- or two-strap slippers with or without heels, some having bows.

French-type all-bisque generally have good flesh color tinted bisque and are artistically painted. Many have kid lined joints so the bisque will not rub together, and many will have tiny cork pates.

Germany's Kestner firm seems to have produced more all-bisque dolls than any other Germany company. Here are a few clues to Kestner made dolls: A great number will have the domes of the head warped out of shape, the top lip is painted "squared" off at the ends, they have glossy multi-stroke eyebrows with upper and lower black eyeliner and many have lower painted lashes only (some have upper painted lashes also). Kestner liked blue-grey eyes and used plaster pates. He also liked one-strap shoes with a pom-pom on the toe and the shoes are generally black with yellowish soles. A great number of Kestner all-bisques have unpainted socks with a blue band at the top, but he also used pink vertical ribbed socks with no top band or rose and magenta bands. He also used blue vertical ribbing with dark blue bands as well as blue circular ribbing with no top band.

Some of the Kestner mold numbers for all-bisque dolls are: 112, 130, 142, 150, X150, 151, 152, 164, 192, 208, 257, 307, 310, 314, 600, 620.

The following is a desirability rating for all-bisque dolls:

French (identified)	Peg jointed
French-type in original clothes	Glass eyes, swivel neck with
Jointed knees and elbows	molded hair
Slender legs	Arms not alike (molded in same
Long stockings (above knees)	position
Pierced ears	Free standing thumbs
Kid in joints	

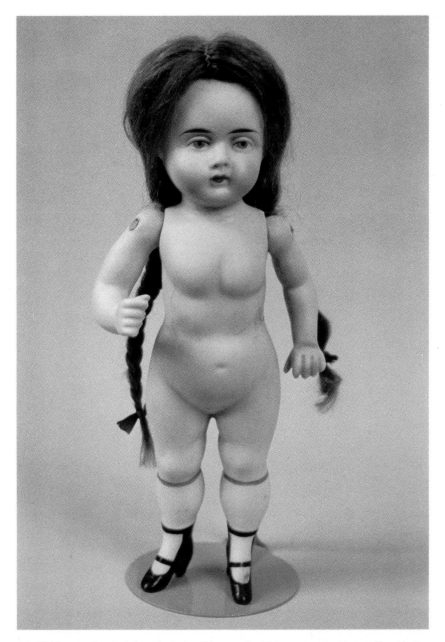

9″ All-bisque that is jointed at shoulders only. The arms are strung then holes are pegged with wood. Very fine body and arm detail to modeling. Painted-on socks with black tops, black heeled boots with two straps. The head is just slightly turned, eyelids are molded, and there is a rather sad look to the face. The eyes are painted. (Author). $225.00

All Bisque

8″ ''Flapper'' style all-bisque jointed at shoulders and hips. Has long thin limbs, painted features and original wig. The dress may be original. Painted on ''Mary Jane'' black shoes and legs are painted tan to just above the knees (hose). Eyes are painted to the side and she has a closed smile mouth. Has extremely well defined and modeled hands. Marks: Germany, across back. (Author). $365.00

4½" - 5" "Bonnie Babe" and "Baby BoKaye". Both are all-bisque with painted-on shoes and socks and both are all original. The "Bonnie Babe" has an open mouth with sideward smile and the "Baby BoKaye" has a closed mouth. "Bonnie Babe" was designed by Georgine Averill and heads were produced in Germany. The "Baby BoKaye" was designed by J. Kallus of Cameo with heads made in Germany. Courtesy Pauly Deem. Bonnie Babe - $825.00. Baby BoKaye - $1,300.00.

4" All-bisque girl incised: Germany, on back. Original wig, set brown eyes, closed mouth and painted black one-strap shoes with white knee high socks edged in blue. Jointed hips and shoulders. 5½" all bisque girl incised: 100, on back crown edge. Original blonde wig, sleep blue eyes, open mouth with two molded teeth. Jointed shoulders and hips. Painted-on shoes and socks with tan color soles. Courtesy Florence Maine. 4" - $165.00. 5½" - $195.00

All Bisque

5" Bisque head with glass eyes. Original wig and possibly original clothes. Painted-on black socks and yellowish brown shoes. Marks: 13, on head. Composition five-piece body. Courtesy Rosalind Cranor. $245.00

1½" All-bisque doll with molded, painted hair, painted features, jointed at shoulders and hips and has painted-on shoes and socks. Wire runs into doll's body and into the horse's body so doll is not removable. Original ''Bare back'' rider's costume. The horse is papier mache and has original trappings. (Author). $265.00

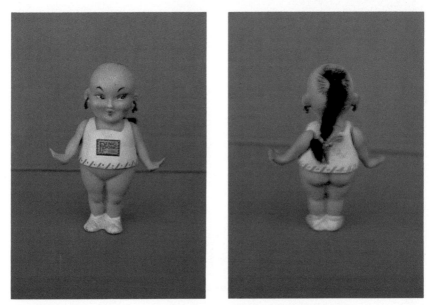

4½" ''Ping Pong'' all-bisque and made in Germany in 1920. One piece body, head and legs. Jointed at shoulders. Wig is ''plugged into'' head. Paper label states: Courtesy Pauly Deem. $95.00

All Bisque

4″ All-bisque with glass eyes. Looks like original clothes. Original wig, and has painted-on black "Mary Jane" shoes. Courtesy Rosalind Cranor. $165.00

4½″ All bisque with glass eyes, closed mouth and painted-on black stockings with green shoes. Has numbers on back which may be: 91, plus "Made in Germany". The wig is original and possibly the clothes. Courtesy Rosalind Cranor. $165.00

All Bisque

5″ "The Little Imp" all-bisque jointed at shoulders and hips. Hoofed feet, star-shaped hands. Marks: The Little Imp/Copyright G.B. & Co. Germany. Courtesy Kimport Dolls. $245.00

3⅞″ Tall with glass eyes in bisque swivel head. Rest of doll is also bisque, and the costume could be original. Has painted-on shoes. Original wig. Courtesy Rosalind Cranor. $200.00

4″ All-bisque with glass eyes, original wig, painted-on shoes and socks. Marks: Made in Germany, on back. Courtesy Rosalind Cranor. $165.00

4″ All-bisque with swivel neck, painted features and marked on shoulders: 40.0½. Pink painted-on socks with black shoes. Courtesy Rosalind Cranor. $200.00

4″ All-bisque with glass eyes, original wig and clothes. Painted-on white socks and black shoes. Unmarked. Courtesy Rosalind Cranor. $145.00

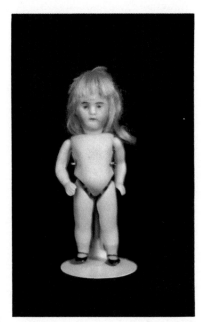

4½″ Tall all-bisque with painted features. Marked: 401, on back. Swivel head and jointed at hips and shoulders. Original wig. Painted-on yellow socks and shoes. Courtesy Rosalind Cranor. $200.00

Armand Marseille (A.M.)

There is a great variety of quality to the Armand Marseille dolls. They can be very poor quality in the detail of the artists' painting or they can compare with the finest of the German makers. The finer the bisque (pale, not highly colored or "smeared" looking) the higher price the doll will be.

The Armand Marseille factory began in 1865 in Koppelsdorf, Thuringia, Germany, with the majority of their dolls being made in the 1890's and into the 1920's. They were always proud of their dolls and the dolls will be fully marked. Sample marks:

```
590
A. 5 M.,
Germany
D. R. G. M.
```

```
ARMAND MARSeille
     GERMANY
        390
   A   7/0   M
```

A great number of the Armand Marseille dolls are still around because, of the German makers, they exported a greater amount of dolls and also supplied the replacement head market with vast quantities of their heads (to retailers and wholesalers).

The dolls by Armand Marseille must be judged, not because they are A.M. dolls, but on the QUALITY OF THE INDIVIDUAL DOLL'S WORKMANSHIP.

Armand Marseille made some very interesting character molds and these are very rare with most being of excellent quality. They may be wigged or have molded hair; some have intaglio painted eyes while others have glass eyes. Some will have fully closed mouths and others open/closed mouths:

Mold #248: 10" - $625.00	14" - $825.00	17" - $1200.00
#372 Kiddijoy: 14" - $525.00	17" - $825.00	
#550: 10" - $825.00	16" - $1,600.00	20" - $2,000.00
#560a: 10" - $400.00	16" - $600.00	20" - $800.00
#590: 10" - $525.00	16" - $1,300.00	20" - $1,800.00
#600: 10" - $700.00	16" - $1,500.00	20" - $1,900.00
#360: 14" - $375.00	18" - $625.00	
#500: 10" - $375.00	16" - $725.00	20" - $1,200.00

ADULT FACE mold numbers: 400 & 401 with long thin jointed limbs with knees jointed higher on legs:

14" - $800.00	16" - $1,300.00	20" - $1,800.00

ADULT FACE mold number 400 and 401 with painted bisque heads:

14" - $400.00	16" - $700.00	20" - $1,000.00

BABIES WITH MORE UNCOMMON MOLD NUMBERS such as: 328, 329, 352:

10" - $265.00	14" - $350.00	22" - $500.00

Same mold numbers on toddlers bodies:

14" - $450.00	22" - $650.00

BABY GLORIA:

14" - $475.00	18" - $700.00	24" - $950.00

FANY (mold numbers 230 & 231);

14"- $2,200.00	18" - $3,300.00	24" - $5,000.00

FANY on toddler body:

17" - $3,400.00	20" - $4,100.00	22" - $4,700.00

GOOGLIES: Mold Numbers 254, 320, 210 and others with intaglio eyes:

7" - $495.00	12" - $1,100.00

#310 (Just Me) with fired-in color:

9"- $900.00	12" - $1,200.00

310 (Just Me) with painted bisque:

9"- $385.00	12" - $600.00

#323 with glass eyes (Most common A.M. googly):

7" - 625.00	12" - $850.00

BABIES WITH MORE COMMON MOLD NUMBERS: Can be on composition, bent limb baby bodies, or have cloth bodies.

#341 with closed mouth and #351 with open mouths are "MY DREAM BABY" made for the Arranbee Doll Company. There are babies with the mold number 345-Kiddiejoy that are the same as the 351 mold number doll:

6"-7" - $165.00	14" - $350.00	24" - $795.00
9" - $200.00	16" - $450.00	
12" - $275.00	20" - $600.00	

#341, 351 & 345 with fired-in brown or black bisque:

9" - $265.00	16" - $525.00	23" - $800.00
12" - $425.00	19" - $700.00	26" - $1,100.00

CHARACTER BABIES with mold numbers: 327, 971, 985, 990, 992, 995 & 996:

14" - $300.00	22" - $525.00
18" - $475.00	26" - $750.00

Armand Marseille

TODDLER BODIES:
14" - $400.00	22" - $625.00
18" - $575.00	26" - $850.00

FLORADORA: Composition body:
9" - $165.00	18" - $350.00	28" - $575.00
14" - $225.00	24" - $465.00	32" - $675.00

FLORADORA: On kid body:
14" - $200.00	24" - $445.00
18" - $325.00	28" - $550.00

QUEEN LOUISE: Composition body or kid body:
10" - $185.00	18" - $400.00	28" - $650.00
14" - $350.00	24" - $500.00	32" - $725.00

370 mold number, on kid body with bisque socket head or bisque shoulder head:
14" - $145.00	26" - $425.00	40" - $1,300.00
16" - $225.00	30" - $550.00	
22" - $325.00	36" - $950.00	

390 mold number on composition, jointed body:
14" - $165.00	26" - $450.00	40" - $1,500.00
16" - $250.00	30" - $575.00	
22" - $350.00	36" - $1,000.00	

1890, 1894, 1897, 1914, etc. mold numbers:
12" - $250.00	22" - $500.00	40" - $1,600.00
15" - $325.00	30" - $625.00	
18" - $400.00	36" - $1,100.00	

12″ Tall with 12″ head circumference. Head is marked: 126 2½ Germany. Has high colored bisque head and open pursed mouth with two tiny teeth, and is very similar to the Armand Marseille "Just Me". The doll has been referred to in two ways, as a "Just Me" baby, and as a "Patsy Baby". Lightly molded hair, and comes with set or sleep eyes. Courtesy Elizabeth Burke. 12″ - $325.00. 16″ - $995.00.

Armand Marseille

9″ Googly incised: Armand Marseilles/Germany/323 A 6/0. Has blue googly eyes, closed smile mouth and is on excellent quality five-piece papier-mache body. All original except shoes and socks. Courtesy Florence Maine. $725.00

19″ "Fany" with 11½″ head circumference. Unusual composition body with straight wrists. Blue sleep eyes, closed mouth and extremely pouty face. Marks: 231/Fany (in script)/A. 7M. A very rare Armand Marseille baby. Courtesy Elizabeth Burke. $3,400.00

Armand Marseille

13″ Tall with 9″ head circumference Armand Marseille character child on a composition toddler body with voice box in back. Fine quality bisque head with blue sleep eyes, open/closed mouth with molded tongue. The toddler body has one-piece arms and legs. Marks: 251/G.B./Germany/A.).M./DRGM 248/1. The doll was made for George Borgfeldt by Armand Marseille. Courtesy Elizabeth Burke. $475.00

14″ Marked: A.M. 390. Dressed in original Oriental costume. Has elaborate hair style, grey set eyes, open mouth with four teeth. Is on fully jointed composition body. Courtesy Florence Maine. $165.00

Armand Marseille

Left to right: "Tia" (with red lei) is 8″ tall and is a 341 Armand Marseille with closed mouth and sleep eyes. Big doll is "Samoa" and incised: 2½. His body is embossed: Sch. 4. He is 13″, has sleep eyes, and is on a toddler body. Next is "Tawny", who is 8″ tall and also a 341 Armand Marseille. From the collection of Jimmy & Faye Rodolfos. 8″ - $225.00. 13″ - $475.00. 18″ - $685.00

15" Socket head on five-piece bent leg baby body. Sleep eyes, open mouth with two lower teeth. Bald head (closed dome) and marked: A.M./Germany/351.14.K. This is the open mouth version of "My Dream Baby" made by Armand Marseille for Arranbee Doll Co. 1924. From the Lori Bates Collection. $350.00

Armand Marseille

24" "My Dearie" marked: Made in Germany/Armand Marseille/DRGM 946/1 390n. Sleep eyes with lashes, open mouth with four teeth and on fully jointed composition body. Holding all original character-faced tin head baby with composition hands and partial arms ending in wire under clothing. Has no real body, but has large working squeeker inside. Painted hair where it shows, painted blue eyes and open/closed mouth with two teeth. Courtesy Florence Maine. $465.00

7" Bisque head with glass eyes and open mouth. Five- piece composition body, original wig and clothes. Marks: Germany/390/A 13/O M. Made by Armand Marseille. Courtesy Rosalind Cranor. $100.00

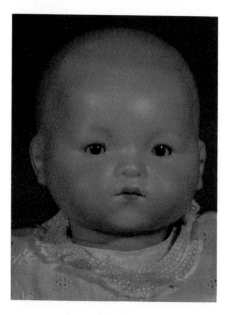

16" Armand Marseille "Dream Baby" made for the Arranbee Doll Co. Mold number 341. Sleep eyes and on five-piece bent leg baby body. Courtesy Kimport Dolls. $450.00

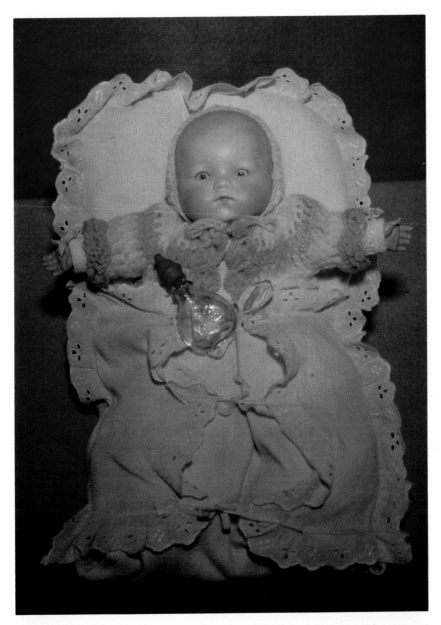

"My Dream Baby" with 10" head circumference, sleep eyes, closed mouth and incised: A.M. only, but cloth body is stamped: 20732. Celluloid hands, cry box. Dressed in original knit undershirt with pink ribbons and flannel diaper and laying on original white pique, eyelet trimmed bunting/pillow tied with pink ribbons. It is not a hand puppet type Dream Baby, although the bunting/pillow reminds one of them. Courtesy Florence Maine. $225.00

Armand Marseille

14″ Crying "Dream Baby" made by Armand Marseille. Cloth body with composition hands, blue glass eyes. A cute character baby. Courtesy Elizabeth Burke. $565.00

14″ Tall with 6½″ head circumference. Bisque head with sleep eyes and a closed mouth character. The body is an adult lady composition body with molded bust line, jointed elbows and knees and is called a "Flapper style" body. Marks: Armand Marseille/Germany/401/A 5/0 M. Courtesy Elizabeth Burke. $800.00

16″ Character baby on five- piece toddler body. Head is incised: 971 A 6 M Drgm 267. Original wig. sleep eyes, open mouth with two teeth. Courtesy Florence Maine. $425.00

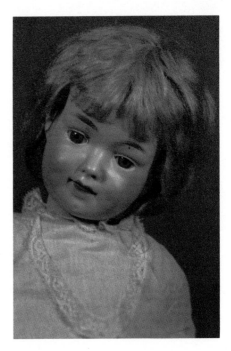

18″ Bisque head marked: 590/A.5M./ Germany/DRGM. Has open/closed mouth and original baby wig. On five-piece bent leg baby body. Courtesy Kimport Dolls. $1,400.00

Armand Marseille

18" "My Dearie" made for George Borgfelt, open mouth and character face with slight smile. Marked: Made in Germany/Armand Marseille/390n D.R.G.M. 246/1/A 2½ M. Center: 18" with open mouth, character face with smile and marked: Made in Germany/A Baby 2 Betty M/D.R.G.M. Made by Armand Marseille for Butler Bros. 18" "Dorothy" with sleep eyes, open mouth and six tiny teeth, smiling face. Marked: Made in Germany/560a/A3M/D.R.G.M. 232/1. Courtesy Reins Collection. 18" - 390N - $350.00. 18" Baby Betty - $400.00. 18" 560a - $700.00

5⅛" Bisque head with sleep eyes and on five-piece composition body with slender limbs, painted-on shoes and socks. Marks: A. 16/O. M. Made by Armand Marseille. Courtesy Rosalind Cranor. $165.00

Armand Marseille

16" Marked: 1894 AM 1 DEP, on bisque head. Crude wooden, fully jointed body. Set eyes and open mouth with four teeth. Courtesy Florence Maine. $350.00

7½" Armand Marseille marked: A.M. with painted bisque head, glass eyes and open mouth. On five-piece body. Dressed as Russian Bride. Courtesy Kimport Dolls. $100.00

13½" Marked: 1894/A.M. 2 Dep. Made by Armand Marseille. Set eyes, open mouth and on composition and wood jointed body with "stick" legs. Stick legs have very long upper legs, jointed at knees and short lower legs. May be original wig. One stroke eyebrows. (Author). $265.00

18″ Marked: Made in Germany/Floradora/A.5M. Has sleep eyes, open mouth with four teeth and is on jointed composition body with straight wrists. All original clothes and wig. Courtesy Pat Timmons. $350.00

ALT, BECK & GOTTSCHALCK

Alt, Beck & Gottschalck opened a porcelain factory called Porzellan-fabrik Von Alt in 1854. They were among the producers of both the Bonnie Babe and Bye-lo babies for George Borgfeldt Co. You will often find that dolls from this firm, with same mold number, can be found on a baby body or on a fully jointed body. (Example: mold number 1361 or 1367, etc). MARKS:

BABY DOLLS: 1909 into 1920's. Open mouth, sleep or set eyes, pierced nostrils and on bent limb baby body:

12″ - $350.00	20″ - $550.00
15″ - $400.00	25″ - $795.00
17″ - $495.00	

TODDLER BODY OR FLIRTY EYES:

15″ - $500.00	20″ - $650.00	25″ - $895.00

CHILD DOLL: Open mouth, sleep or set eyes and on fully jointed body:

16″ - $295.00	24″ - $425.00	36″ - $875.00
21″ - $365.00	30″ - $700.00	40″ - $1,300.00

30″ Marked: A.B.G. on fully jointed composition body, has open mouth and set eyes. May be original wig. Courtesy Diane Hoffman. $700.00

AMBERG, LOUIS & SONS

Louis Amberg began business in 1878 and continued into the late 1930's. He was a major doll importer and operated from both New York City and Cincinnati, Ohio. The most well-known doll by Louis Amberg was "New Born Babe" designed by Jeno Juszko in 1914. The Bye-lo baby came on the market in 1924 (distributed by George Borgfeldt), and Amberg re-issued the "New Born Babe".

Sample marks:

L, A. & S. 1914
G 45 520

19 © 24
LA & S NY
GERMANY
- 40 -
982/4

BABY PEGGY MONTGOMERY: Mold #972, 982, socket or shoulder head, fully closed mouth:
18" - $2,600.00   22" - $2,900.00

BABY PEGGY MONTGOMERY: Mold number 973, 983, socket or shoulder head with smiling mouth (closed):
18" - $2,800.00   22" - $3,200.00

BABY PEGGY MONTGOMERY: All bisque with closed smiling mouth, molded hair with full bangs and in "Dutch" bob. One piece body and head and painted molded-on Mary Jane shoes and white socks: 6" - $400.00
NEW BORN BABE: Marks: L.A. & S. 1914/G45520 with some marked: "heads copyrighted by Louis Amberg". Cloth bodies, can have composition, celluloid or rubber hands. Bisque heads with painted hair, sleep eyes and closed mouth with slightly protruding upper lip;
14" - $500.00   18" - $850.00

NEWBORN BABE: Open mouth. Marked: L.A. & S. 371.
14" - $425.00   18" - $625.00

Amberg, Louis

22" Tall with 10" head circumference. Bisque head has brown sleep eyes, closed smiling mouth with dimples. Original "Dutch" bob wig, kid body with bisque lower arms. Marks: 1924/L.A.&S. N.Y./ Germany/-50-/983/2. Made for Louis Amberg and Son. Courtesy Elizabeth Burke. $3,200.00

16" "New Born Babe" with bisque head, cloth body and celluloid hands. Sleep eyes and closed mouth. Marks: L.A. & S. 1914/#G45520/Germany. Made for Louis Amberg and Son. (Author) $595.00

AVERILL, GEORGENE

Georgene Averill was the wife of James Paul Averill and involved in the companies of Madame Georgene Dolls, Paul Averill Manufacturing Company, Averill Manufacturing Company, Georgene Novelties, and was artist and designer for George Borgfeldt as well.

"Madame Hendren" was a line of dolls manufactured by the Averill Manufacturing Company in the United States and the Brophey Doll Company in Canada. Sample marks:

Copr. by
Georgene Averill
Germany
1005/3652
1402

BONNIE BABE: All-bisque has open mouth, molded hair, glass eyes and is jointed at neck, shoulders and hips. Has paper label on chest: 5"-6" - $825.00

BONNIE BABE: Bisque head with open mouth and two lower teeth, molded hair, cloth body with composition lower arms and often legs, but can have all cloth legs:
15" - $750.00   20" - $1100.00

WONDER BABY: Mold number 1400. Bisque head on cloth body with composition or celluloid hands. Closed mouth:
15" - $925.00   20" - $1,200.00

21" "Bonnie Babe" with 15" head circumference. Solid dome bisque head, flanged neck, brown tinted hair and brown painted lashes top and bottom. Blue sleep laughing eyes, open "lop-sided" smile mouth with two porcelain teeth. Muslin body with composition arms and legs, and turned up big toe. Marks: Copr. by Georgene Averill/1005/3652. Courtesy Margaret Mandel. $1,250.00.

BAHR & PROSCHILD

Bahr & Proschild had a porcelain factory located in Ohrdruf, Thuringia, Germany. The first records of the company were in 1871 and their first dolls were china heads. Then they began making bisque and by 1910, they also made celluloid doll heads and parts. Sample marks:

CHARACTER CHILDREN: Will have closed mouth, sleep eyes and on a fully jointed or toddler body:
15" - $2,220.00   18" - $2,800.00

BABIES: Mold numbers 535, 585, 604, 619, 624, 678, etc.:
10" - $345.00   22" - $675.00
14" - $400.00   25" - $800.00
18" - $550.00

TODDLERS: With same mold numbers as the BABIES:
10" - $445.00   22" - $775.00
14" - $500.00   25" - $900.00
18" - $650.00

10¾" Bisque socket head on five-piece bent limb baby body. Set blue eyes, smile open mouth with two molded-in teeth. Original wig and shoes and socks. Marks: B' ✗ P/585   2/0   Germany. Courtesy Jo Fasnacht. $345.00

20″ Baby made by Bahr and Proschild with mold number 604/5. Sleep eyes and open mouth. Courtesy Jay Minter. 10″ - $345.00. 20″ - $600.00

Bahr & Proschild

This little girl is a "smiler". Just 14″ tall, with an open/closed mouth and four painted upper teeth. Her eyes are intaglio and brown. The body is fully jointed and she is all original. We think someone just told her she was going to the zoo! She is marked: B P 4 (incised) and belongs to Marlowe Cooper. This delightful child took a First Prize (Blue) at the Milwaukee Convention. 14″ - $2,100.00

BERGMANN, C.M.

C.M. Bergmann opened a factory in 1889 and by the year 1909, he had a factory at Walterhausen and one at Friedrichroda, both in Germany. He made dolls on ball jointed bodies, as well as kid bodies. Many of his bisque heads were made for him by such companies as Armand Marseille, Simon and Halbig, Kestner and others. The marks often carry the full name of C.M. Bergmann, but some have the initials of C.M.B. along with the name of the maker of the bisque head. Sample marks:

SIMON+HALBIG
C.M.B
GERMANY
1916

C.M.BERGMAN
il
WALTERHAUSEN
Germany

BABIES: Open mouth, sleep or set eyes, wigged, on five piece bent limb baby body:

10" - $200.00	14" - $395.00	18" - $595.00

TODDLER BODIES:

14" - $495.00	18" - $695.00

BABY: Mold number 612:

14" - $495.00	18" - $695.00

CHILD DOLL: On fully jointed body, open mouth, set or sleep eyes:

14" - $195.00	24" - $475.00	36" - $1,300.00
18" - $325.00	30" - $725.00	40"-42" - $1,600.00

Bergmann, C.M.

18″ Character baby on five-piece composition bent leg baby body. Set blue eyes, open mouth with four upper teeth. The wrists of this baby body are jointed. Bisque head circumference is 13″ and doll has a cork pate. Original bobbed wig and marked: Simon Halbig/C.M. Bergmann/612. Head made by Simon and Halbig for C.M. Bergmann. Courtesy Alice Metherd. $795.00

BORGFELDT, GEORGE

George Borgfeldt was the largest importer working in the United States and he had locations in England, Canada, Germany, Bavaria, New York City and Vienna. Dolls were made for the Borfeldt firm by Alt, Beck & Gottschalck, Armand Marseille, Simon & Halbig, Kling and many others. It is not known for certain if the dolls marked with just the "G.B." stands for George Borgfeldt, or not, but they are attributed to him by collectors.

CHILD DOLL: On fully jointed body, open mouth and set or sleep eyes:
14" - $195.00   24" - $475.00
19" - $375.00   30" - $725.00

Both 24" dolls are marked: Made in Germany/G.B. Have original brown wigs, blue sleep eyes with lashes, open mouths and original clothes. These two dolls were made for George Borgfeldt and were owned by twin girls. Courtesy Pat Timmons. $475.00 each

CENTURY DOLL COMPANY

The Century Doll Company was located in New York City and was a distributor of dolls; their bisque heads were made by Kestner of Germany. They were known to have operated from 1909 to 1925. Sample marks:

CENTURY DOLL C?
KeStner Germany

⬦ⓀGERMANY -
CeNTURY

CHARACTER BABIES: Solid dome bisque head, lightly molded or set or sleep eyes, painted hair, closed or open/closed mouth, cloth body with composition or celluloid hands:
13" - $525.00   15" - $625.00   18" - $750.00

MAMA TYPE DOLL: With bisque shoulder head that is a child style face instead of a baby face, on kid or cloth body. Open mouth, set or sleep eyes:
16" - $350.00   20" - $550.00   24" - $700.00

Century Doll Company

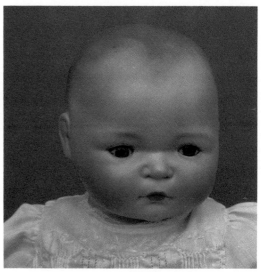

18″ Century baby with bisque head, sleep blue eyes, closed mouth and painted hair. Head circumference is 13″. Cloth body, composition arms and jointed at hips with tin discs. Marks: Century Doll Co./ Kestner Germany. J.D. Kestner made the head for the Century Doll Co. Courtesy Alice Metherd. $750.00

16″ Bisque head on cloth body with composition hands. Sleep eyes and closed, pouty mouth. Marks: 1924/E.I. Horsman/ Made in/Germany. The head was made by Century for the Horsman Company. (Author) $550.00

Century Doll Company

17″ Baby marked: Century Doll Co./Kestner Germany. Molded curl on forehead, along with slightly molded hair. The eyes are brown and set; she has an open/closed mouth with two modeled teeth. Cloth body with disc jointed shoulders and hips. Wears original gown. Courtesy Jill Koons. The Century Doll Co. operated from 1909-1925. They were located in New York City and made a great many dolls with composition heads. It was in 1925 that they had Kestner (Germany) make up bisque heads for them. $750.00

CHINA

China is glazed porcelain and has been made since 1750, but did not reach top popularity until the 1840's. The hair-do usually reflects the times of the dolls, but not always, as the makers sometimes continued to make a certain hair-do long after the hair trends had changed. One of the "carry overs" was the flat top style with short curls all around the head shown in the 1862 London Exhibition. Dolls with that hairstyle were still being made in 1884.

Most of the very early china heads have long necks and very adult hair-dos, and the rarer child types of the same period had shorter necks and short hair styles. One child type has corkscrew curls all around the head and being a very popular hair style, dates from the 1840's through the 1870's.

Considered rare in china heads are: boys, head bands, flowers, combs, painted brown eyes, glass eyes, snoods, a swivel neck, pierced ears or a bald head made for a wig.

Almost all china heads had black hair, but during the 1880's, blondes became more popular and by 1900, one out of three of the common type china with wavy hair (called "low brow" or "Butterfly" hair-do) was a blonde.

Known makers of china heads were Kling, Hertwig, Kestner, Closter, Bahr & Proschild and Japan (during W.W.I). In the U.S. there were many distributors of china dolls including George Borgfeldt, Butler Brothers and Morimura Brothers.

"Pet name" china heads have names stamped in gold letters along the yoke of the chest. These chinas were: Agnes, Bertha, Daisy, Dorothy, Edith, Esther, Ethel, Florence, Helen, Mabel, Marion, Pauline, and there may be others. The "Pet Name" chinas were made from 1905 to the 1930's. They all have the "Common", "Butterfly" and also called "Low Brow" style hair-do.

China

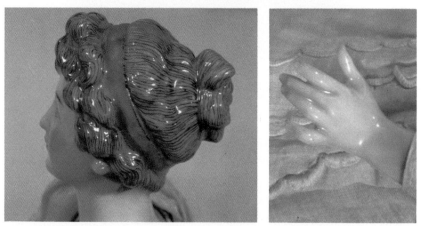

12″ Early china made by Nymphenburg firm located near Munich, which was the State Porcelain factory of Bavaria ca. 1799-1830. Wood flat feet and long thin legs, delicate detailed china lower arms and exquiste detailed hands with rest being cloth. Apollo knot hairdo with green band, brown painted, detailed eyes, Empire cut gown, modeled bust and marked ⊕ inside shoulder plate. The back of shoulder plate is very detailed in modeling also. (Author). $1600.00

17" China ca. 1860's with blonde hair and black head band, fully exposed ears and high swirl curls. Molded eyelids and original clothes. Cloth body with "spoon" china lower arms, flat feet with molded-on boots. Notice the way the curls are formed and the extreme care in modeling the ears. Made in Germany with porcelain maker's mark inside the shoulder plate. (Author) $800.00

14″ Ballerina that is all china glazed and jointed only at the shoulders. Molded feet in ballerina toe position and has very fat upper legs. Hands are very delicate. The eyes are modeled in a ''looking down'' angle and a space was left un-painted between the lips. Molded brownish brush stroke hair with yellow and black beading on top. Molded bust. Part of original costume. There was a triple layer of fine net-like material under the tutu that brought the entire costume down to just below the knees. (Author). $550.00

21″ Wigged china of 1880's. Cloth body with china lower arms and legs. Extremely detailed modeled hands. Old, beautiful clothes. (Author). $895.00

19″ Bald head china, no sew holes and crown is unglazed. Old body that has been re-covered to preserve it, china lower limbs. Courtesy Kitty Best. $750.00

China

21″ Fancy hairdo china with cafe au lait hair with molded pink and yellow roses, blue forget-me-nots and green leaves. Two sew holes, old cloth body with old china lower limbs. Courtesy Kitty Best. $1,000.00

14″ Blonde china with child-like face, two sew holes, old cloth body with brown leather mitt-type hands and stitched-on leather books. Marks: Germany 159. Made in Germany by Kling. Courtesy Kitty Best. $400.00

DRESSEL, CUNO & OTTO

The Dressel firm was founded in 1700, but up to 1863, not much is known about them except they made wood and papier mache toys. Otto Dressel, Sr., along with his sons, are listed as doll makers in 1873. In 1875 they registered the "Holz-Masse" in Germany. They purchased bisque heads from many different factories, such as Armand Marseille, Simon & Halbig, etc.

Cuno and Otto Dressel (.C.O.D.) began using the "Jutta" trademark in 1906 and by 1911, they were also making celluloid heads. In 1914, much of their factory at Sonneberg burned, but they rebuilt and reopened in 1915. Besides the doll factory, there were two toy factories with one in Nurnburg and the other in Grunhainichen. Sample marks of the Cuno & Otto Dressel Company are:

"HoLZ MASSE"

CHARACTER DOLL: With closed mouth, glass eyes and on jointed body:
14" - $1,800.00   17" - $2,600.00

ADULT BODY LADY: Slim waist, long thin limbs, molded bust and feet molded to wear high heel shoes. Bisque head with closed mouth and glass eyes:
13" - $950.00   16" - $1,200.00

CHILD DOLL: Composition jointed body, open mouth, glass eyes:
14" - $265.00   21" - $375.00
17" - $300.00   25" - $525.00

CHILD DOLL: On kid body with bisque lower arms, open mouth, glass eyes:
14" - $225.00   21" - $345.00
17" - $275.00   25" - $495.00

BABY: Bisque head with molded hair or wig, glass eyes and open mouth. On five-piece bent limb baby body:
14" - $325.00   17" - $450.00   21" - $525.00

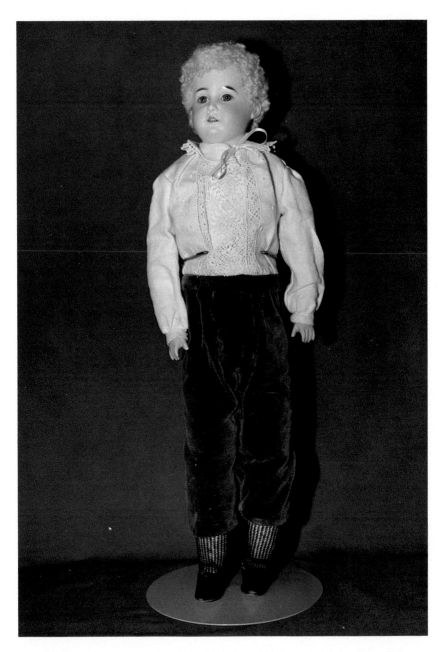

20½" Bisque head marked: C O D 93-2 Dep. The head and shoulder plate are in one piece, on kid body with bisque lower arms. Open mouth. Courtesy Pat Timmons. $375.00

Dressel, Cuno & Otto

26″ Toddler with socket head. Open mouth and sleep eyes. Marks: 1349/Jutta/S & H. Head made by Simon and Halbig for Cuno & Otto Dressel Co. (Author). 20″ - $525.00. 26″ - $700.00

GOEBEL, WILLIAM

William Goebel is the son of Franz Dellev Goebel and has used the "bee" mark since 1879. Sample marks:

GOOGLY: Painted eyes to the side, five-piece mache body with painted-on shoes and socks: 5"-6½" - $625.00

MOLDED FLOWERS IN HAIR: Girl with molded hair and flowers, five-piece mache body with molded-on shoes and socks: 6" - $325.00. 10" - $495.00

CHILD DOLL: Open mouth, glass eyes, and on jointed body:
12" - $165.00	20" - $395.00
16" - $295.00	24" - $495.00

WALKER: With bisque head and on walker body:
14" - $245.00	17" - $325.00

6" Goebel-made bisque head with molded hair with molded flowers. Painted eyes, open/closed smiling mouth with painted upper teeth. Five-piece papier mache body with painted-on shoes and socks. Marks: Courtesy Pauline Hoch.
$325.00

17" Bisque head with wood and papier mache walker body. Straight legs. Set eyes, open mouth with teeth. Marks: R/13/Ox/Germany, on one side of neck and: , on the other side. Courtesy Pauline Hoch. $325.00

HALF DOLLS

Half dolls called "pin cushion" dolls by most collectors can be of bisque, china glazed, composition, papier mache or terra cotta. Not all were used for pin cushions, but for items such as lamps, tea cozies, candy boxes, powder boxes and perfume bottles.

Most half dolls date from 1900 on into the 1930's with the majority of them made in Germany, although many were also made in Japan. If marked, they generally will only have a number and the country of origin. The most desirable will be marked with the company, such as William Goebel ( ) or Dressel, Kister & Company ( ).

The best half dolls have the arms and hands molded completely away from the body (not touching the body), will have jointed shoulders, bald heads with wigs, and portray children or men.

Arms & hands completely away from body:

5" - $125.00   8" - $200.00   12" - $600.00

Arms extended but with hands attached to figure:

3" - $65.00 up   5" - $85.00 up

Common figures with arms and hands attached to figure: 3" $22.50 up

MADE IN JAPAN:

3" - 15.00 up   5" - $22.50 up

7" Tall bisque half doll with painted-on mask, excellent detailed painted blue eyes and beauty spot. Original wig. Both hands have delicate modeling and are molded away from body. Marks: , incised on top in back and also same mark, along with ✗, artist mark in blue on the inside. Made by Wm. Goebel. (Author). $695.00

HEINRICH HANDWERCK

Heinrich Handwerck was located in Gotha near Walterhausen, Thuringia, Germany in 1876. They made dolls and doll bodies although they used some heads made for them by Simon & Halbig and other companies.

Some of the distributors for Handwerck dolls were Nerlich & Co., George Borgfeldt, B. Illfelder, Foulds & Freure, Davis & Voetsch. Their dolls were being sold as late as 1927. Sample marks:

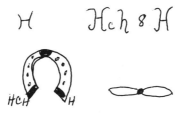

CHILD DOLL: Bisque head with open mouth, glass eyes and wig. Fully jointed body:

14" - $225.00	26" - $575.00	40" - $1,500.00
18" - $375.00	30" - $700.00	
22" - $450.00	36" - $1,200.00	

MOLD NUMBER 109 & 119: Also others with oversized large expressive eyes:

18" - $400.00	24" - $500.00	30" - $750.00

30" Heinrich Handwerck incised: H 109 15 DEP with original wig, glass sleep eyes, open mouth with four teeth and pierced ears. On fully jointed composition body with a stamp in red: Heinrich Handwerck Germany 6. Courtesy Florence Maine. $750.00

Heinrich Handwerck

17½" Heinrich Handwerck incised: 79 10 Germany H 2. Original wig, sleep eyes, open mouth with two teeth and on fully jointed composition body. Pierced ears. Courtesy Florence Maine. $375.00

20″ Heinrich Handwerck incised: 119 10 ½ X Handwerck/Germany 2 ¼. Sleep eyes, open mouth with six straight cut teeth of porcelain, on fully jointed body and has pierced ears. Courtesy Florence Maine. $450.00

HEUBACH, GEBRUDER

The Heubach Brothers (Gebruder) made dolls from 1863 into the 1930's. Their factory was at Lichte, Thuringia, Germany. They started making character dolls in 1909 or 1910. Often the bodies of these later dolls will be rather crude, but the quality of the head makes up for the lack of quality in the bodies. Sample marks:

CHARACTER DOLLS: Bisque heads, open/closed mouth, intaglio painted eyes and on jointed or five-piece mache bodies. ALLOW MORE FOR GLASS EYES:

MOLD NUMBER: 5636: Laughing child:
10"-12" - $1,000.00   17" - $1,850.00

5777 & 9355: "Dolly Dimples":
16" - $1,200.00   22" - $2,200.00

5730: "Santa": 20" - $1,800.00

6736: Laughing child with wide open/closed mouth, modeled lower teeth:
10"-12" - $750.00   17" - $1,500.00

6969, 6970, 7246, 7407, 8017, etc: Boy or girl pouty with fully closed mouth:
12" - $1,400.00   16" - $1,700.00   20" - $2,500.00

7604: Laughing child:
10"-12" - $325.00   14"-15" - $595.00   18" - $725.00

7622: Molded-hair pouty:
10"-12" - $650.00   15"-16" - $1,100.00

7788: "Coquette", tilted head, molded hair and can have molded flowers or ribbons in hair:
12" - $700.00   16" - $1,600.00
7977: "Baby Stuart," has bisque bonnet:
10"-12" - $1,000.00   Glass eyes - $1,500.00
14"-15" - $1,500.00   Glass eyes - $1,900.00

8192: 14" - $525.00
17" - $650.00   20" - $750.00

8774: "Whistling Jim" has eyes to side and mouth modeled open in whistling position:
12" - $750.00   16" - $1,000.00

BABIES OR INFANTS: Bisque heads, molded hair or wigs, bent limb baby bodies and open/closed pouty mouth. Can have intaglio or sleep eyes:
8" - $275.00   10" - $325.00

PORTRAIT INDIAN: Man or woman: 13" - $2,600.00
MOLD NUMBER 119 (along with 1867): Braids coiled around ears:
16" - $1,800.00

CHILD DOLLS: Open mouth, glass eyes and on jointed body:
16" - $425.00   19" - $595.00   24" - $695.00

MOLD NUMBER 10633: "Dainty Dorothy" with open mouth:
16" - $450.00   20" - $575.00   25" - $695.00

GOOGLY:
8" - $825.00   12" - $1,350.00   14" - $1,550.00

Heubach, Gebruder

10½″ Girl incised: 8192 Germany Gebruder Heubach 8/0. Grey sleep eyes, open mouth with four teeth. Is on very nice fully jointed composition body. Courtesy Florence Maine. $300.00

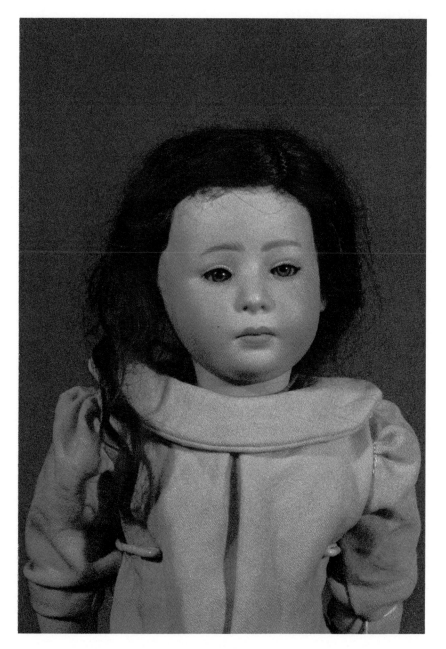

16″ Pouty Gebruder Heubach with bisque head on fully jointed composition body. Closed mouth and glass sleep eyes. Courtesy Kimport Dolls. $1,700.00

Heubach, Gebruder

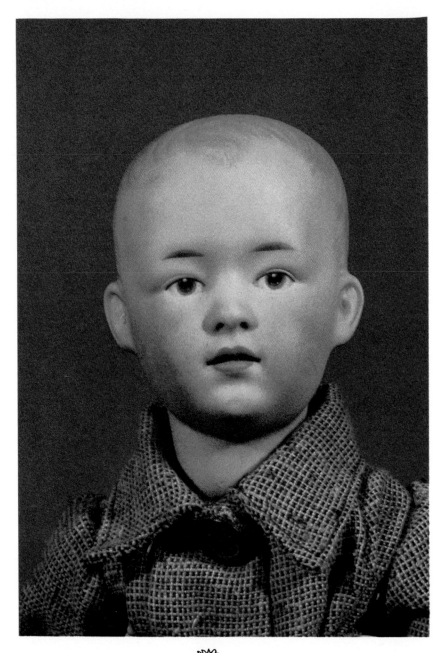

13″ Gebruder Heubach marked: 🌱 13 Germany. Closed mouth, painted intaglio eyes, on composition jointed body. Courtesy Kimport Dolls. $850.00

20″ Incised on head, "Heubach", brown eyes and open mouth with two lower teeth that gives her the appearance of laughing. This size is rare. The Heubach Brothers (Gebruder Heubach) were one of the largest makers of character children. This doll was a Blue Ribbon winner, plus Gold Cup for Favorite of Show. Courtesy Marlowe Cooper. 12″ - $1,000.00. 20″ - $2,200.00

HEUBACH KOPPELSDORF

Ernst Heubach operated from his factory in Koppelsdorf, Thuringia, Germany from 1887, and by 1895 had over 100 people working for him. Some Heubach dolls will be marked with the full name and the mold numbers where others may be marked:

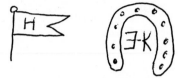

CHARACTER BABIES: Bent leg baby bodies with mold numbers 300, 320 (White), 342 etc. Allow more for Flirty Eyes or Toddler Body:

12" - $325.00	20" - $525.00
16" - $425.00	26" - $750.00

CHILD DOLL: Open mouth, sleep eyes, jointed body and often found with mold number 250:

10" - $165.00	24" - $425.00
14" - $245.00	30" - $800.00
20" - $345.00	

CHILD DOLL: Open mouth and on kid/cloth body. Bisque shoulder head and often mold number 275:

14" - $195.00	24" - $375.00
20" - $295.00	30" - $750.00

BLACK OR BROWN DOLLS: Mold numbers 320 or 399:

10" - $350.00	16" - $600.00
12" - $400.00	20" - $800.00

NEWBORN STYLE INFANT: Painted hair, sleep eyes and closed mouth. On cloth body with celluloid or composition hands:

12" - $375.00	16" - $495.00

CHARACTER INFANT: Mold number 339 or tan fired bisque head toddler with mold number 452:

12" - $395.00	15" - $500.00

CHARACTER CHILD: Bisque shoulder head, open/closed mouth, molded hair and on cloth/composition body.

12" - $400.00	16" - $695.00

8″ Marks: Heubach Koppelsdorf/250. 18/0/Germany. Blue sleep eyes, original brown mohair wig, open mouth with four teeth and on five piece composition body with painted-on white socks and molded-on brown shoes. Courtesy Penny Pendlebury. $140.00.

Heubach, Koppelsdorf

13″ Original "Skater". Bisque head, sleep blue eyes, blonde wig, open mouth with four teeth. The body and limbs are stuffed silk. Her original costume is white trimmed in gold and hat is trimmed with real fur. Marks: Germany/275.18/0./Heubach Kopelsdorf. Courtesy Jo Fasnacht. $245.00

9″ Child doll with blue bow in hair, open/closed mouth and painted eyes. Marks: 282-18/0/E.H. Germany/DRGM. Made by Ernst Heubach. Courtesy Kimport Dolls. $375.00

Heubach, Koppelsdorf

22″ Painted bisque head with sleep eyes and on a five-piece toddler body of papier mache. Head marked: Heubach Koppelsdorf 342.2 Germany. Clothing could be original and wears an early synthetic wig. Courtesy Sally Freeman. $375.00

12½" Socket head on composition bent leg baby body. Brown sleep eyes, closed mouth and dome head with wash painted hair. Original. Marks: Heubach Koppelsdorf/ 399. 6/0/Germany/D.R.G.M. Courtesy Lori Bates. 12½" - $400.00. 18" - $725.00

9½" Heubach Koppelsdorf 399 14/0 DEP. brown baby in original grass skirt. Courtesy O.D. Gregg. 9½" - $350.00. 16" - $600.00

Heubach, Koppelsdorf

11″ Incised: Heubach Koppelsdorf 471-14/0 Germany. Original blonde mohair wig, original sunsuit and hat. Five-piece jointed body of good quality papier mache, blue sleep eyes, closed mouth. No painted lashes and feathered eyebrows. Very highly colored bisque. Courtesy Florence Maine. $195.00

JENSEN, HELEN

"Gladdie the Laughing Child" was designed in 1927 and was on the market in 1928-1929. The head can be made of a ceramic material which is painted, or of fired bisque. The body is cloth and limbs are composition. Modeled from the two year old daughter of Helen & Holger Jensen, but doll will most often be found dressed as a boy. Marks:

Gladdie

Copyright By
Helen W. Jensen

PAINTED CERAMIC HEAD: 17"-18" - $875.00
FIRED BISQUE HEAD: 17"-18" - $2,000.00

18" Bisque head with molded hair, laughing half-closed eyes and wide open/closed mouth with molded upper teeth. Cloth body with composition limbs. Rare doll with a bisque head as most are of a ceramic, painted material. Courtesy Shirley Bertrand. $2,000.00

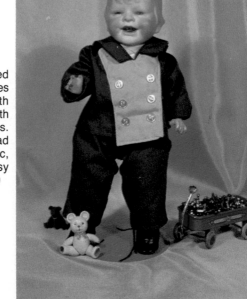

Jensen, Helen

17″ "Gladdie The Laughing Child". Head made of ceramic type material which is painted. Molded, painted hair, sleep laughing eyes and open/closed mouth with modeled upper teeth. Cloth body with composition limbs. Marks: Gladdie/copyright by/Helen W. Jensen. (Author). $875.00

Full view of "Gladdie". The composition arms are rather short. This costume is not old, but looks good on the doll. (Author).

KAMMER AND RINEHARDT

Kammer and Reinhardt started in 1886 and continued into the 1930's. They bought out the Heinrich Handwerck factory in 1902 and most of their doll heads were made by Simon & Halbig. In 1916 Kammer and Reinhardt stock was sold to Bing Works (marks: G.B.N., B.W. & BIN.) who was one of the largest German toy manufacturers and had as many as 4000 employees. They kept Mr. Reinhardt in the capacity of advisor-counselor and by 1933, 95% of this stock was owned by Eichorn & Sons.

Kammer and Reinhardt have used the trademark of K star R since 1895 and "Mein Liebling" (My Darling) from 1901. In 1901, Ernst Kammer, modeler and creator of their dolls, died and was replaced by Karl Krauser.

In 1909 Kammer & Reinhardt introduced a line of character dolls such as mold number 100 "Baby" mistakenly referred to as "Kaiser Baby". It must be remembered the bent limb baby body was very new and the Kaiser of Germany was born with a slight deformity. The doll came from Germany and so a connection was made someplace along the line and the doll is still called "Kaiser Baby". The mold number 101 came as a boy (Peter) or girl (Marie). In 1910 came mold number 107 (Carl), 109 (Elise) and a boy or girl 114 (Hans and Gretchen). Kammer and Reinhardt advertised that all these molds were designed after real children.

It wasn't until 1920 that mold number 126 was used and it is the most frequently found. Mold number 116 looks very much like the Kestner "Hilda", yet number 116/A has an entirely different look with close set eyes, dimples and an open/closed mouth. Other mold numbers followed the same pattern, such as the 117 with a closed mouth "pouty" look, yet the 117A has an exceptional "sweet face" look. The 117N has an open mouth, and the 717 is the mold 117N made in celluloid with heads made for them by Rheinische Gummi & Celluloid Fabric Co.

Sample marks:

K✡R
Simon + Halbig
117

CHARACTER BOY OR GIRL: Mold number 101 with painted eyes:

9" - $1,000.00	14" - $1,800.00	17" - $3,000.00

102,107,109,112:

16" - $7,500.00 up	20" - $9,000.00 up

114: 9" - $1,200.00	14" - $2,600.00	17" - $3,900.00

117-117A:

16" - $3,200.00	20" - $3,800.00	24" - $5,000.00

101 With glass eyes:

14"- $2,200.00	17" - $3,400.00

117N: Open mouth:

16" - $800.00	20" - $1,400.00

123-124:

16" - $6,500.00	20" - $10,000.00 up

Kammer & Rinehardt

CHARACTER BABIES: Open/closed or closed mouths. Mold number 100: "Kaiser Baby":
10" - $475.00   16" - $650.00   18" - $900.00
100-Black or tan bisque:
10" - $900.00   16" - $1,200.00
115-115A: 15" - $2,500.00
18" - $2,700.00   22" - $3,200.00
116-116A: 15" - $2,000.00
18" - $2,300.00   22" - $2,900.00
118: Open mouth: 16" - $650.00
20" - $1,000.00
118A: Closed mouth: 18" - $1,600.00
22" - $2,000.00

BABIES: Add more for flirty eyes. Open mouths. Mold numbers 121,122,128:
14" - $600.00   18" - $850.00   22" - $995.00
TODDLERS: 14" - $850.00
18" - $1,100.00   22" - $1,500.00
126: 12" - $400.00
15" - $525.00   20" - $725.00
TODDLER: 16" - $625.00
20" - $800.00   24" - $1,000.00
127 TODDLER: 16" - $800.00
20" - $1,500.00
MOLDED HAIR BOY: Open mouth:
15" - $475.00   22" - $825.00
MOLDED HAIR BOY: Open/closed mouth:
15" - $995.00   22" - $1,350.00

SMALL CHILD DOLLS: Open mouths and on five-piece bodies:
5" -$200.00   8" - $295.00

CHILD DOLLS: Open mouth. Often with mold numbers 400,403,109,etc. Add more for flirty eyes:
16" - $425.00   26" - $650.00   40" - $2,000.00
18" - $475.00   30" - $800.00
22" - $500.00   36" - $1,450.00

GOOGLY: Mold number 131:
12" - $3,900.00   15" - $6,500.00   17" - $7,500.00

CELLULOID BABIES: With kid or kideleen or cloth bodies. Open mouth:
15" - $275.00   20" - $395.00

CELLULOID CHILD: Open mouth. Mold numbers such as 225, 255, 321,406,717,826,828,etc: Jointed bodies:
16" - $450.00   20" - $575.00

9½"-9¾" Marked: L/Simon Halbig/K ✡ R/ Germany/23. Five-piece composition bodies, bisque heads and painted-on shoes and hose. Called "Sewing Dolls" of the 1920's. Child made the costumes with the organdy and crepe paper that came with the dolls. Courtesy Pauly Deem. $200.00

Kammer & Rinehardt

10″ Tall and called by collectors, "Kaiser Baby". The mold number is 100 and he was made by Kammer and Rinehardt (K star R). The light brown fired in bisque head has brush stroke hair and painted brown eyes and open/closed mouth. This brown #100 is very, very rare and is generally found in white bisque. Courtesy O.D. Gregg. 10″ - $900.00. 15″ - $1,200.00

19″ "Marie" Kammer and Rinehardt mold number 101 pouty. Has 11″ head circumference. Composition ball jointed body. Blue painted eyes, closed mouth and had very good quality bisque. Unusual in this size. Courtesy Elizabeth Burke. $3,200.00

Kammer & Rinehardt

15″ Marked: K  R/Simon & Halbig/115/A/38. Socket head with closed pouty mouth, sleep eyes and on wood and composition toddler body. Courtesy Reins Collection. $2,500.00

16" "Moritz" is also a character from the cartoon books of Wilhelm Busch of Germany (1832-1908). She has molded on brown shoes and unusual blue eyes. Her marks are: 124/Simon Halbig/K Star R. Schoenhut also made a "Moritz" doll. Max and Moritz are extremely rare character dolls and, generally will be found only in company of a very advanced collector. Courtesy Marlowe Cooper. $6,000.00 up

Kammer & Rinehardt

Large life-size 25″ Kammer and Rinehardt baby with 19″ head circumference. Composition jointed body, original gown, blue sleep eyes and open mouth with tongue sticking out, two upper teeth. Marks: K star R/126/Made in Germany. Courtesy Elizabeth Burke. $1,800.00

24" Character baby with 16" head circumference. Bisque socket head on bent limb baby body, brown sleep eyes, painted lashes top and bottom, feathered eyebrows, open mouth with two teeth, and dimples. Marks: K star R Simon & Halbig 122. Made for Kammer and Rinehardt by Simon and Halbig. Courtesy Margaret Mandel. $1,100.00

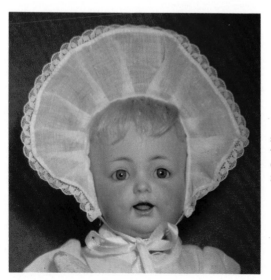

15" Baby marked: K star R 10N 11/11A 122. Original wig, sleep eyes, open mouth with two teeth and tremble tongue. Courtesy Florence Maine. $675.00

Kammer & Rinehardt

11″ Marked: K star R 114. Painted eyes, closed pouty mouth and on fully jointed composition body. Made by Kammer & Rinehardt. A gift from author's best and dearest friend. $1,300.00

14″ Kammer and Rinehardt boy incised: K star R 114/43. Intaglio, painted eyes, closed mouth and sparce remains of original wig. Dressed in old black wool sailor suit and hat. Fully jointed composition body. Courtesy Florence Maine. $2,600.00

22″ Tall with 12½″ head circumference "Mein Liebling" with closed smile mouth, blue sleep eyes and on fully jointed composition body. Marks: K star R/Simon & Halbig/117/A. The head was made by Simon & Halbig for the Kammer and Rinehardt firm. Courtesy Elizabeth Burke. $4,600.00

Kammer & Rinehardt

23" Marked: K ✡ R/717/58 Germany. Celluloid socket head with open mouth and flirty eyes with tin eyelids and on "Flapper" style jointed body. 20" K ✡ R/Simon & Halbig/117/50 with sleep eyes, closed mouth and on jointed body. 18½" K ✡ R/Simon & Halbig/117/a/50 with closed mouth and sleep eyes. 15" K ✡ R/Simon & Halbig/117n with open mouth, flirty eyes with tin eyelids, jointed body with rubber hands. Courtesy Reins Collection. 23", 117 - $4,700.00. 20", 117 - $3,500.00. 15", 117N - $750.00

In blue: 16½" marked: K ✡ R/Simon & Halbig/117/43. Socket head on jointed body. Closed mouth and sleep eyes. Center: 17" marked: K ✡ R/Simon & Halbig/117n/Germany. Socket head on jointed body, blue flirty eyes with tin eyelids, open mouth with four teeth. In yellow is 13" marked: K ✡ R/Simon & Halbig/117/A/36. Socket head on jointed body, sleep eyes and closed mouth. Courtesy Reins Collection. 16½"-17" - $3,200.00. 13", 117 - $3,300.00

18″ Kammer and Rinehardt baby. Sleep eyes and original wig. Marks: K star R/Simon & Halbig/128/42. Courtesy Mary Partridge. 14″ - $600.00. 18″ - $850.00

Kammer & Rinehardt

15″ Flirty eyed girl marked: K star R/717/39/Germany and is the celluloid version of the 117n "Mein Leibling". Wig is replaced as are the clothes. Open mouth with four teeth. Jointed five piece body and has glass, flirty eyes with the patented "naughty" eyes where metal lids close part way when laid down to one side (naughty girl) and all the way when laid down on other side (good). Registered in 1915 as "Der Unart" (The Naughty One) and referred to as "My Rosy Darling". Courtesy Florence Maine. $450.00

15″ Incised: K Star R/Simon Halbig/131. Closed, smiling mouth that is a line and huge blue eyes. She is on a jointed toddler body and is completely original. Two types of these googlies are seen; this one with spike eyebrows, and the other with regular eyebrows. She was a Blue Ribbon winner at the San Diego Convention, now in the collection of Marlowe Cooper. $6,500.00

KESTNER, J.D.

Johannes Daniel Kestner of Walterhausen, Thuringia, Germany, made all kinds of dolls and bodies. They made entire dolls and were one of the few German makers that did. In 1895 Kestner registered their trademark of the crown and streamers in the U.S., and in 1896, they registered the same trademark in Germany. This trademark is found on the dolls' bodies. Kestner was in business as early as 1804, but began making dolls in 1845. They began making heads of porcelain (bisque) and china by 1860.

The Ladies Home Journal had a series of paper dolls created by Sheila Young called "Lettie Lane's Real Doll "Daisy"". The only way to get the real doll was to sell three subscriptions, at least one renewal and two new ones, plus $4.50. The promotion included the doll and patterns that followed the paper dolls. In April, 1911, "Lettie Lane's Most Beautiful Doll as a Bride" was introduced in July, 1911, came "Lettie Lane's Doll in Vacation Clothes", and December, 1911, added "Lettie Lane's Most Beautiful Doll in her Party Clothes".

The first order for the dolls was 5,000 but they were gone in a short time and two factories had to be used for a total of 26,000 additional dolls before the close of the offer in January, 1912. The "Lettie Lane" paper doll's "real live doll" "Daisy" was the Kestner with the mold number 174, and the Kestner 171. When additional dolls were ordered, they also included the Kestner mold number 154. With over 31,000 dolls given out in the U.S. as late as 1911, it is understandable why the 154, 171 and 174 mold numbers are the most likely to be found and are referred to as common mold numbers.

During 1915 Kestner registered two more Crown trademarks in Germany. One carries the words, "Kronen Puppe" and the other "Crown Doll/Kestner/Germany".

Most Kestner dolls are marked with sizes that include a letter and a number, for example, C-7, F-10, D-8. Sample marks:

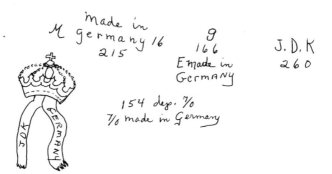

CHILD WITH CLOSED MOUTH: Kid or composition jointed body. Mold number X and other pouties:
14" - $1,400.00   17" - $1,700.00   20" - $1,900.00

CLOSED MOUTH MARKED XI: Composition jointed body, straight wrists:
14" - $1,550.00   17" - $1,800.00   20" - $2,000.00

CLOSED MOUTH: Marked only with size number:
14" - $1,200.00   17" - $1,500.00   20" - $1,800.00

TURNED SHOULDER HEAD: Closed mouth. Mold numbers such as 169, 639, 698, 969, etc.:
17" - $950.00   20" - $1,100.00   24" - $1,500.00

TURNED SHOULDER HEAD: Open mouth:
17" - $375.00   20" - $500.00   24" - $625.00

CHARACTER CHILDREN: Closed mouth, or open/closed mouth. Mold number 208 with painted eyes:
17" - $2,700.00   22" - $3,200.00
212: Glass eyes: 14" - $2,000.00
17" - $3,100.00   20" - $3,600.00
224: Open mouth: 16" - $495.00
241: Glass eyes: 16" - $1,900.00   20" - $2,800.00
249: 20" - $1,000.00
260-257 CHILD OR TODDLER:
16" - $650.00   20" - $850.00
BOXED SET COMPLETE DOLL AND THREE EXTRA HEADS: $4,800.00. Extra heads from sets on old bodies. (Allow more for glass eyes). Mold numbers 175, 176, 177, 178, 179, 182, 184, 185, 186, 190, 212, etc.
12" - $1,600.00   16" - $2,300.00
ADULT: Mold number 162: 17" - $950.00
GIBSON GIRL: Mold number 172: or marked on body:
12" - $1,200.00   17" - $1,700.00   21" - $2,850.00

CHARACTER BABIES: Open mouth, wigged or molded hair. Numbers 142, 150, 151:
12" - $400.00   16" - $500.00   20" - $700.00
152: 12" - $400.00   16" - $500.00   20" - $700.00
211, 226:
14" - $475.00   20" - $700.00
237, 245, 1070 HILDA:
12" - $2,700.00   16" - $2,700.00   20" - $3,200.00

Kestner, J.D.

HILDA TODDLER:
16" - $3,300.00   20" - $3,700.00   23" - $4,200.00

243 ORIENTAL:
14" - $2,200.00   18" - $2,800.00

247: 12" - $625.00   16" - $1,200.00
257: 12" - $450.00
16" - $625.00   20" - $800.00   26" - $1,100.00

GOOGLY: Mold number 221:
12" - $4,000.00   14" - $4,800.00

CHILD DOLL: Open mouth, composition jointed body or kid body and may
have fur eyebrows. Mold numbers 129, 143, 145, 146, 147, 159, 162, 164,
166, 167, 168, 192, 196, 215, 264, etc:
14" - $375.00   20" - $600.00   36" - $1,500.00
17" - $500.00   26" - $700.00   40" - $1,800.00

CHILD: with mold numbers 154, 171, 174:
15" - $375.00   22" - $495.00
18" - $450.00   27" - $700.00

TRUNKS WITH WARDROBES:
9" - $550.00   12" - $750.00   14" - $950.00

TINY DOLLS: Open mouths and jointed bodies:
7" - $250.00   9" - $300.00

26″ Baby with dimples and pale blue eyes. She has an open mouth and is on a five-piece bent leg baby body. The marks are: Made in Germany/152. Made by Kestner. Courtesy Jay Minter. 12″ - $400.00. 18″ - $650.00. 26″ - $1,000.00

Kestner, J.D.

19″ Kestner marked: Made in Germany/6½.168.7½. Socket head on wood and composition body. Sleep eyes and open mouth. 19″ marked: IV/154/6 bisque socket head with molded, painted hair, sleep eyes and closed mouth. On wood and composition jointed body. This "Tommy Tucker" version is attributed to Kley and Hahn. Courtesy Reins Collection. 19″, 168 - $525.00. 19″, 154 - $2,400.00

26″ J.D. Kestner with composition ball jointed body and beautiful smooth bisque. Open mouth with four upper teeth, brown eyes and molded eyebrows. Marks: K½ Made in Germany 14½/171. Original boy style, side part wig. Courtesy Elizabeth Burke. $675.00

Kestner, J.D.

15½″ Boy with bisque head marked: 179. Brown painted eyes, open/closed mouth with molded tongue. Dressed in old sailor suit (hat added) and has original wig. On fully jointed composition body. Made by J.D. Kestner. (Author). $2,300.00

14½″ Bisque head marked: 182. Original wig, old clothes. Closed mouth with brown painted eyes. On fully jointed composition body. Made by J.D. Kestner. (Author) $2,000.00

Kestner, J.D.

16½″ "Hilda" with sleep eyes, open mouth and two upper teeth. On five piece Kestner toddler body. Bisque head made by Kestner and is marked:

(handwritten mark:)
Made in 73
Germany
237
J. D. K. JR. 1070
1914
©
HILDA

$3,300.00

16½″ "Hilda" full length, on toddler body, original wig and old clothes with coat missing. (Author).

This beautiful 26" "Hilda" baby by J.D. Kestner is in the collection of Cynthia Orgeron. Photo by Neil & William Venta. 14" - $2,000.00. 20" - $3,200.00. 26" - $4,400.00

Kestner, J.D.

14″ Kestner Oriental with 10″ head circumference. Very fine toned olive bisque, dark brown sleep eyes, open mouth and two teeth. Kestner baby body and original old clothing with jade pin in center of costume. Marks: J.D.K./243/Made in Germany. Courtesy Elizabeth Burke. $2,200.00

18″ Marked: Made in Germany/J.D.K./257. Bisque head with rare flirting brown eyes, open mouth with two upper teeth and tongue showing. Original fur wig and on bent limb baby body. Courtesy Elizabeth Burke. $700.00

15½" Marked: Made in Germany/J.D.K./260/Germany/34/37.40. Bisque socket head with sleep eyes, open mouth with porcelain teeth and on jointed body. Right: 18½" marked: 985/Germany/A.3 M. Socket head on jointed body with open mouth and two teeth. Has dimples in cheeks. Courtesy Reins Collection. 15½" - $400.00. 18½" - $475.00

18″ J.D. Kestner Gibson Girl. Closed mouth. Clothes are extremely well made. Marks: Made in Germany. Courtesy Kimport Dolls. $2,550.00

Kestner, J.D.

10″ J.D. Kestner bisque head baby with open mouth, molded gum line on top and ONE tiny tooth on bottom. Brown sleep eyes, original blonde human hair wig. Head circumference is 8″. Composition bent leg baby body. Marks: Made in Germany/211/J.D.K. Courtesy Elizabeth Burke. $275.00

Kestner Googlies mold #221. There were six sizes made, #5, 6, 7, 10, 11,12. Sizes 8 and 9 have not turned up yet. All have sleep eyes, some brown and some blue. All have jointed toddler bodies with some having the straight wrists and others jointed wrists. Mouth is straight line closed watermelon shape, eyebrows slanted, curving up at nose and going downward. Left to right: #5, 6, 7, 10, 10, 11,12. Courtesy Marlowe Cooper. 12″ - $4,000.00

15″ Marked: 149 Made in Germany C-7. Made by J.D. Kestner. Sleep eyes, heavy feathered eyebrows and open mouth. On fully jointed composition body. $400.00

Kestner character baby incised: 257 Made in Germany 41. Blue sleep eyes with real hair upper eyelashes, open mouth with two teeth and tremble tongue. Very highly colored bisque and is on five-piece bent leg baby body. Courtesy Florence Maine. 16″ - $625.00

Seated: 16″ marked: DEP 154½. One-pin-jointed kid body, has brown sleep eyes, open mouth with two teeth. Standing: 13″ incised: 154 and is on a gussetted kid body with the Kestner crown and streamers mark stamped on it. Sleep eyes, open mouth with two teeth molded in. Courtesy Florence Maine. 16″ - $400.00. 13″ - $285.00

Kestner, J.D.

This baby boy is marked: J.D.K./Made in 11 Germany and was made by Kestner. He has an open mouth and is on a bent leg baby body. The eyes are brown and sleep. Courtesy Penny Pendlebury. 8″ - $285.00. 15″ - $500.00. 19″ - $700.00. 22″ - $1,000.00

KLEY & HAHN

Kley & Hahn operated from a porcelain factory in Ohrdruf, Germany from 1895 to 1929. Some of the Kley & Hahn character dolls are extremely fine dolls and rather difficult to find. These are the children with closed, or open/closed mouths and painted eyes. Sample marks:

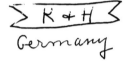 K + H *Walküre*

CHARACTER CHILD: Boy or girl with molded, painted hair or wigs, closed or open/closed mouths. Intaglio eyes (add more for glass eyes). On jointed or toddler body. All 500 (except 585) series mold numbers:

12"- $1,500.00	20" - $4,000.00
16" - $2,500.00	24" - $4,400.00

CHILD DOLL: Open mouth, jointed body. Mold number 250, along with the mark: Walkure. The Walkure mark can be found without the mold number 250 also:

16" - $295.00	24" - $625.00	32" - $1,100.00
20" - $495.00	28" - $725.00	

BABIES: Open/closed mouths, five-piece baby body (add more for toddler body). Mold numbers 130, 142, 150, 199:

12" - $495.00	20" - $825.00
16" - $595.00	24" - $1,100.00

BABIES: Open mouths. Mold numbers 132, 162, 167, 176, 585:

12" - $400.00	16" - $500.00	20" - $650.00

Kley & Hahn

24″ Kley and Hahn with the K & H in banner and no mold number. Jointed toddler body and head has well defined features. Open/closed mouth and glass eyes. Courtesy Marlowe Cooper. $4,500.00

18″ Marked K & H 134/5. Made by Kley and Hahn. Character doll with glass eyes and fully closed mouth. On fully jointed composition body. Courtesy Kimport Dolls. $2,900.00

Kley & Hahn

18″ Marked: K & H/167-6. Has open mouth with two teeth and tongue. On fully jointed composition body. Made by Kley and Hahn, Germany. Courtesy Reins Collection. $595.00

24″ Kley and Hahn 520. This one has a bald head (closed dome) but they also come with sliced crowns. Intaglio blue eyes, closed mouth and fully jointed body. These Kley and Hahn character children are rare and a great addition to any collection. Courtesy Marlowe Cooper. $4,400.00

Kley & Hahn

21″ Kley and Hahn character child marked: 526 K & H. Closed mouth, painted intaglio eyes and unpierced ears. Original clothes. Ball jointed composition body marked: Germany. Original wig. Ca. 1912-1914.   (Author). $4,000.00

Full length view of Kley & Hahn character child with mold number 526 to show original gown and wig. (Author).

16″ Marked: 536/4. Made by the Kley and Hahn firm of Germany. Came as either boy or girl. These character children by the Kley and Hahn factory are outstanding, and as with all character dolls, are very desirable. Intaglio eyes and closed mouth. On fully jointed composition body. Courtesy Pauly Deem. $2,500.00

19½″ Marked: K & H 526 with brown painted eyes, full closed mouth and sweet expression. Courtesy Kimport Dolls. $3,900.00

KLING

Kling & Company of Ohrdruf, Thuringia, Germany made dolls from 1880 into early 1930's. They made a great many china glazed dolls, but also made porcelain (bisque) dolls. Sample marks:

BISQUE HEAD MARKED WITH KLING (K, inside bell):

16" - $300.00   25" - $695.00
20" - $500.00   30" - $995.00

27" Kling bisque head that is marked on the INSIDE of the head: 737-13/Germany/ . Open mouth, side part wig, applied ears and re-dressed exactly like King Olav of Norway. Kid body with set blue eyes and bisque lower arms. Courtesy Elizabeth Burke. $895.00

Photograph of the real King Olav of Norway complete in state uniform and wears the Order of St. Olav. Courtesy Elizabeth Burke.

LIMBACH

The date Limbach started producing dolls in not known, but it was called Limbach Porzellanfabrik, Limbach, Thuringia, Germany. It is known they made dolls in the late 1890's and early 1900's. Along with the Limbach mark, there may be incised names such as: "Norma", "Willy", "Wally". Sample marks:

CHILD DOLL: Bisque head, jointed body and open mouth.
16" - $325.00   20" - $495.00   24" - $595.00

CHARACTER CHILD: Or toddler, molded hair and open/closed mouth:
12" - $700.00   16" - $1,200.00   20" - $2,000.00

The smaller doll is an 8" Limbach googlie with lips for mouth, straight leg composition body and has bare feet instead of painted-on shoes. Other is 9" Armand Marseille #323 on straight leg toddler body. Courtesy Marlowe Cooper. 8" - $895.00. 9" - $725.00

PAPIER MACHE

Papier mache is made from paper pulp, wood and rag fibers, containing paste, oil or glue. Flour and/or clay or sand is added for stiffness. The hardness of papier mach depends on the amount of glue that is used. The heads are painted with many having a wax over the paint.

M&S SUPERIOR-2015 DOLLS:

14" - $200.00	18" - $400.00	24" - $695.00

GREINER MARKED DOLLS:

23" - $650.00	29" - $1,000.00

18½" Unusual hairdo papier mache of 1830-1840. This one has replaced arms and body using the original sawdust stuffing, but doll has original limbs. The papier mache head and shoulder is "deep" and the elbow to fingers and just above knees to toes are wood carved, with painted-on shoes. Re-dressed. These dolls could have been made in Germany, France or Switzerland. Courtesy Jo Fasnacht. $1,600.00

Papier Mache

Tiny 5" Motschmann style doll with papier mache head overlaid with paint used on head, arms, upper chest area, torso hip area and lower legs. In the center of these parts are muslin sections stuffed with wool dust. Doll has tiny wisps of hair painted over ears and around base of head in back. Original clothes and has tiny glass eyes. (Author). $145.00

7" Circumference Pen Wiper, using the Motschmann style head. May have been made in Germany or Japan, as both countries made similar dolls. Courtesy Jo Fasnacht. $165.00

6¼" Motschmann style doll with glass eyes. Papier mache is painted, head, lower arms and legs, upper chest and torso hip area. Cloth between sections. Courtesy Jo Fasnacht. $145.00

PARIAN

22″ Glass-eyed parian with brownish-blonde wide curls. Pierced ears, cloth body and legs with parian lower arms. Decorated shoulder plate. (Author). $1,500.00

Parian

18½″ Taffy hair parian untinted bisque with molded, applied porcelain flowers and leaves. Painted eyes, pierced ears and extremely curly hairdo. Cloth body with parian lower limbs. (Author). $995.00

17" Brown hair parian with center part and lightly waved hairdo, fully exposed ears and has molded-on shirt top and tie. Dressed as lady, but can also be dressed as a man. Courtesy Kimport Dolls. $995.00

15" Parian with cloth body and parian limbs. Blonde wig and pierced ears. Courtesy Kimport Dolls. $875.00

12¾" Parian with untinted bisque, painted eyes and has molded-on snood with comb in back. Two sew holes, cloth body with parian lower limbs. Courtesy Kitty Best. $550.00

PUTNAM, GRACE STOREY

Grace Storey Putnam was the designer and sculptor of the Bye-lo baby. The first was cast in wax, painted with oil paints that were patted into the wax to give a transparent look. Milio of New York, who worked in wax, made this model and they were sold to Madame Averill (also known as Madame Hendren), and soon Mrs. Putnam was under contract to the George Borgfeldt Company. The dolls were made in all-bisque, rubber, celluloid, composition, bisque and also in vinyl. Grace Storey Putnam obtained copyrights in 1922, 1923 and one in 1925.

The bisque Bye-lo heads were made by various doll makers like Alt, Beck & Gottschalk, Kling, Kestner, Schwab & Co., Hertel, etc. The bodies were made by K & K (Kahl & Kohle) and were distributed by George Borgfeldt. The composition hands were made by the Cameo Doll Company and Karl Stanfuss made the celluloid hands. Wood hands were made by Schoenhut.

Grace Storey Putnam designed other dolls but none were as successful as the Bye-Lo baby. The rarest ones designed by her are the "crying" Bye-lo and "Fly-lo". Marks:

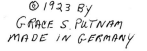

BYE-LO: Measured in head circumference:

10" - $385.00	15" - $685.00
12" - $485.00	18" - $1,300.00

SMILING BYE-LO: 14" - $4,400.00
BYE-LO: On five-piece composition body:
14" - $585.00   17" - $800.00

ALL-BISQUE BYE-LO: Jointed only at hips and shoulders & painted eyes:

Jointed at neck, shoulders and hips, glass eyes: 6" - $600.00.
BYE-LO: Composition head:
10" - $175.00   13" - $300.00   15" - $400.00

BYE-LO: With celluloid head: 14" - $365.00
ALL CELLULOID BYE-LO: 6" - $145.00

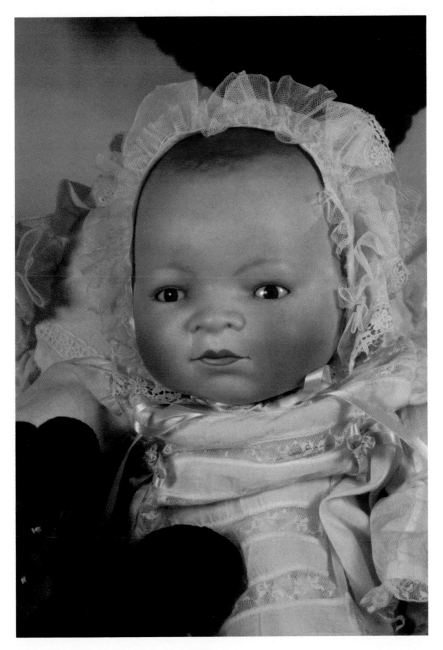

The Bye-Lo baby was called the "Million Dollar Baby" as it was the most popular baby doll ever created. Designed by Grace Putnam in 1923. 18″ Head circumference. Life size. Courtesy Gunnels Collection. $1,300.00

4″ Very hard-to-find wigged, sleep eyed "Bye-lo". All bisque with molded-on socks and pink shoes. Open crown with original blonde wig. Marks on back: Copr. by Grace Storey Putnam/Germany. Head is marked: 16 over 10, also under the arms. Courtesy Elizabeth Burke. $525.00

RECKNAGEL OF ALEXANDRINETHAL

Recknagel of Alexandrinethal started as a hard paste porcelain factory. They produced dolls from 1886 through 1930. Sample marks:

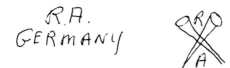

CHILD DOLL: Set or sleep eyes, open mouths and with small dolls having painted-on shoes and socks:

9" - $100.00	16" - $235.00	22" - $425.00
13" - $185.00	19" - $325.00	

CHARACTER CHILD OR BABY: Ca. 1909-1910. Came on five-piece bent limb baby body, toddler body or child body. Sleep or set eyes, open mouth:

12" - $185.00	19" - $325.00
16" - $250.00	22" - $425.00

CHARACTER BABY: Painted eyes, modeled on bonnet, open/closed mouth and may have molded teeth:

8" - $475.00	12" - $545.00

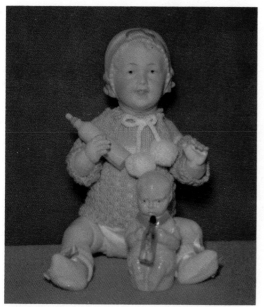

9½" Marked: RA 22-7/0. Made by Recknagel of Alexandrinethal. Molded bonnet head baby with blue intaglio eyes, open/closed mouth with two molded teeth and tongue and on bent leg baby body. Courtesy Florence Maine. $500.00

REINECKE, OTTO

Dolls marked with P.M. were made by Otto Reinecke of Hof-Moschendorf, Bavaria, Germany from 1909 into the 1930's. The most often found mold number from this company is the 914 baby or toddler. The P.M. stands for Porzellanfabrik Moschendorf. Sample marks:

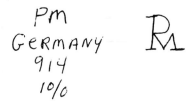

CHILD DOLL: Open mouth, set or sleep eyes, jointed body:
15" - $285.00   18" - $375.00   22" - $450.00

BABY: Open mouth, sleep or set eyes:
12" - $250.00   20" - $500.00
16" - $375.00   25" - $675.00

22" Baby bisque head marked: P.M. 924. On five-piece bent leg composition baby body. Made by Otto Reinecke. Courtesy Kimport Dolls. $525.00

15″ Baby made by Otto Reinecke and marked: P.M. 944/Germany 7. Has sleep eyes and on five-piece bent leg baby body. The "P.M." in the mold mark stands for the name of the factory: "Porzellanfabrik Moschendorf". Courtesy O.D. Gregg. $375.00

SCHILLING

Stephen Max Ferdinand Schilling made dolls in his Sonneberg, Thuringia, Germany, factory from 1884 until 1889 when his son, Ferdinand M. Schilling, took over until 1920. By 1925 the company was run by Max Schilling & Zitzmann. In 1893 they applied for the trademark of a winged angel head over the word "deponirt". Sample mark:

14" "Schilling" that is all original with original dress with Shilling trademark and the words "All wood", on hem of dress. Glass eyes, closed mouth and body is fully jointed. Courtesy Jo Fasnacht. 14" - $1,400.00. 20" - $1,900.00

14″ Schilling doll shown with box end and her other original clothes. Box marked: all wood//1/12 DZ675H/1// Made in Germany//Angel headmark. Courtesy Jo Fasnacht.

Close-up of the wood "Schilling" doll's head, original wig and top of original dress. Courtesy Jo Fasnacht.

SCHMIDT, BRUNO

Bruno Schmidt made dolls from 1900 into the 1930's and operated from Walterhausen, Thuringia, Germany. He not only worked in porcelain, but also in papier mache and celluloid. His trademarks all include hearts, and he registered Mein Goldhertz (My Golden Heart) in 1904 and the BSW in the heart the same year. Sample marks:

"WENDY" MOLD NUMBER 2033: Closed mouth:
16" - $5,000.00 up   20" - $6,500.00 up

CHILD DOLL: Open mouth:
20" - $475.00   24" - $575.00   29" - $995.00

CHARACTER CHILD: Molded, painted hair and eyes and closed mouth:
16" - $2,600.00   20" - $3,200.00

"TOMMY TUCKER" MOLD NUMBER 2048:
16" - $895.00   20" - $1,200.00

BABIES: Wigs and sleep eyes:
14" - $375.00   17" - $485.00   21" - $650.00

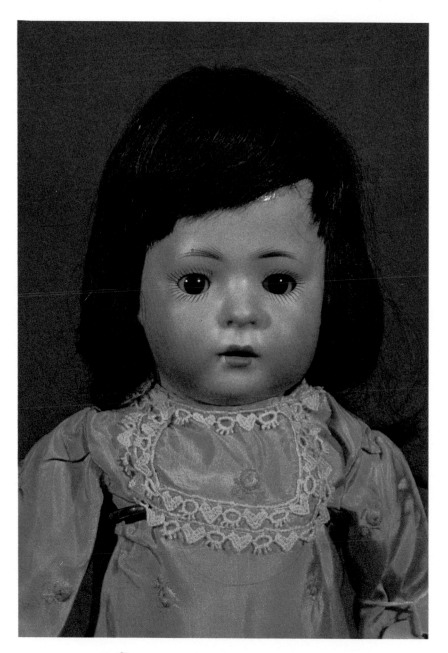

15½″ Marked: (B S / w) /Made in Germany. Bisque head on fully jointed composition body, sleep eyes and open mouth with two upper teeth. Courtesy Kimport Dolls. $700.00

SCHOENAU & HOFFMEISTER

Schoenau & Hoffmeister did not enter the doll making field until 1901 and they were located in Bavaria, Germany. They were also known as Porzellanfabrik Burggrub, and this mark will be found on many of their doll heads. Sample marks:

ORIENTAL: Mold number 4900, open mouth:
10" - $365.00   14" - $895.00   18" - $1,100.00

HANNA: Brown or black bisque, open mouth, grass skirt or native print gown:
8" - $185.00   10" - $250.00

HANNA BABY: Open mouth, white tinted bisque, on bent limb baby body:
16" - $500.00   20" - $600.00   25" - $725.00

PRINCESS ELIZABETH: Smiling open mouth, marked on head:
16" - $2,300.00   20" - $2,700.00   24" - $3,400.00

CHARACTER BABY: Mold number and bent limb baby body, open mouth:
12" - $300.00   20" - $600.00
17" - $525.00   24" - $700.00
TODDLER: 14" - $465.00
17" - $595.00   20" - $695.00

CHARACTER BABY: Closed mouth and sleep eyes:
13" - $550.00   16" - $725.00   20" - $995.00

CHILD DOLL: Mold numbers such as 1909, 5500, 5700, 5800. Open mouths:
10" - $100.00   18" - $395.00   26" - $600.00
15" - $285.00   21" - $425.00

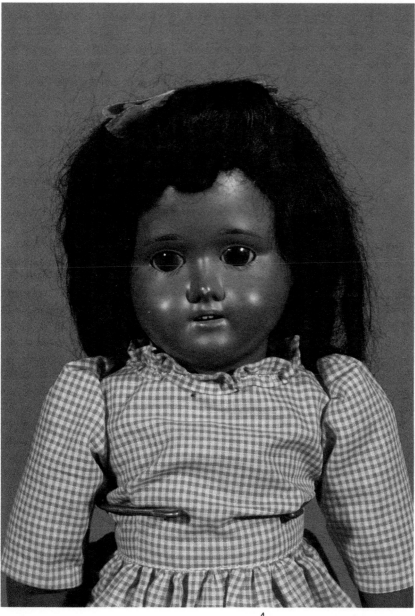

18½″ Black fired-in bisque head marked: /1909. Black fully/ jointed composition body, sleep eyes, open mouth. Courtesy Kimport Dolls. $995.00

18″ Princess Elizabeth, incised along with: Porcellanfabrik Burggrub and Germany. Made by Schoenau & Hoffmeister. These dolls come on two bodies, a toddlers where their head looks much too big for the body and a straight leg body. She has blue eyes, curly short blonde wig and an open/closed smiling mouth with four upper porcelain teeth. Her ears are not pierced. Courtesy Marlowe Cooper. $2,500.00

SIMON & HALBIG

Simon & Halbig operated from sometime in the late 1860's or early 1870's until the mid-1930's. Some of their dolls have molded hair and untinted bisque and quite a few have "bald" heads, which are generally lady-type dolls that were so popular in the 1870's. Simon & Halbig was one of the largest firms in Germany and supplied many heads for other makers such as Fleischmann & Blodel, Kammer & Reinhardt, Cuno & Otto Dressel, Heinrich Handwerck, C.M. Bergmann, Bawo & Dotter, and George Borgfeldt.

In 1895, Simon left the firm (retired or deceased) and Carl Halbig took over as single owner. Carl Halbig did not register the "S & H" until 1905, before that time the dolls were marked "SH" or with the full name "Simon & Halbig". Sample marks:

$$S+H \qquad SH\ 1079\ DEP.$$

HALBIG

☆

Germany

15

SIMON & HALBIG
1299
G.B.

CHILD DOLLS: Open mouths. Mold numbers such as 130, 550, which is most often found, 1009, 1010, 1040, etc., allow extra for flirty eyes:

15" - $385.00	26" - $700.00
18" - $525.00	30" - $995.00
22" - $600.00	

MOLD NUMBER 1079:

15" - $575.00	18" - $675.00	22" - $895.00

CHARACTERS WITH CLOSED MOUTH: Mold numbers 120:
14" -$1,200.00
150, 151: 18" - $5,400.00
153: 18" - $4,600.00
600: 14" - $825.00
718, 719: 16" - $1,800.00
20" - $2,200.00
905, 908; 14" - $1,600.00
17" - $2,600.00

MOLD NUMBERS 939, 949: Closed mouths:
17" - $1,800.00   20" - $2,200.00

Simon & Halbig

MOLD NUMBERS 939, 949: Open mouths:
17" - $750.00   20" - $950.00
MOLD NUMBER 950: 10" - $425.00
MOLD NUMBER 969: 15" - $1,500.00
MOLD NUMBER 1279: 16" - $995.00
MOLD NUMBER 1299: 18" - $925.00
MOLD NUMBER 1388: 20" - $7,600.00
MOLD NUMBER 1428: 20" - $1,600.00
MOLD NUMBER 1448: 15" - 1,800.00
MOLD NUMBER 1488: 20" - $3,900.00
WALKER BODY: Mold number 1039, key wound: 16" - $975.00
LITTLE WOMEN: Mold number 1160:
6" -$300.00   9" - $425.00
ADULT BODY LADY: Mold number 1159, 1179:
18" - $1,500.00   22" - $1.800.00   25" - $2,200.00
LADY: Mold number 1303 with closed mouth; 18" - $5,200.00
MOLD NUMBER 1469: Lady with closed mouth: 18" - $2,600.00
BABIES: Open/closed mouth characters:
15" - $525.00   20" - $800.00

BABY BLANCHE: 20" - $800.00
24" - $1,000.00
SANTA: Mold number 1249:
16" - $575.00   20" - $695.00   26" - $995.00
ORIENTAL: Mold number 1129:
16" - $2,200.00   20" - $2,700.00
ORIENTAL: Mold number 1329:
16" - 1,900.00   20" - $2,400.00

38" Simon and Halbig child with bisque head and fully jointed composition German body. Shown are various sizes of "Bye-lo" babies with very large one being life size. The "Bye-lo" in blue and black are reproductions done in wax by owner. Courtesy Penny Pendlebury. 39" - $1,400.00

Simon & Halbig

18½″ Bisque turned head that is marked: 698. Open mouth, kid body with bisque lower arms. Made by Simon & Halbig. Courtesy Kimport Dolls. $500.00

Left to right: 15″ Marked: Simon & Halbig/K ✡ R/39. Open mouth, flirty eyes with tin eyelids. On jointed composition body. Center: 18″ Gebruder Heubach that is marked with: 5636/"Sunburst" and GH (interwined) DEP/Germany. Inset glass eyes and two lower teeth. 18″ bisque socket head with slightly concave dome and three holes. Closed mouth, glass eyes, kid body with rivited joints and marked: S & H 719 DEP, on head and S & H 720 on shoulder plate. Courtesy Reins Collection. 15″ - $425.00. 18″ - $1,900.00. 18″, #719 - $2,000.00

Simon & Halbig

23″ This extremely rare character girl was made by Simon & Halbig and also carries the mold number 151. She has intaglio blue eyes, open/closed mouth with four painted upper teeth. She has light cheek dimples and fine modeling. Courtesy Marlowe Cooper. $6,200.00

25″ Marked: S&H/949. Open/closed mouth, very large paperweight eyes, heavy painted eyebrows, original wig and old shoes. Made by Simon & Halbig. (Author). $2,600.00

Simon & Halbig

16″ Marked: S & H/949. Closed mouth and set paperweight eyes, on jointed body. Right is marked: 5636/5/"Sunburst" with GH interwined by Gebruder Heubach. She is 16″ tall and on jointed body. Courtesy Reins Collection. 16″ - $1,700.00. 16″, #5636 - $1,700.00

15″ Marked: 969/S & H/DEP. Socket head with inset glass eyes, open/closed mouth and a very smiling character face. She has four peg-like teeth and is on jointed body with straight wrists. Courtesy Reins Collection. $1,500.00

Simon & Halbig

17″ Marked: S & H 1010 with open/closed mouth. Kid body with bisque lower arms. Made by Simon and Halbig. Courtesy Kimport Dolls. $525.00

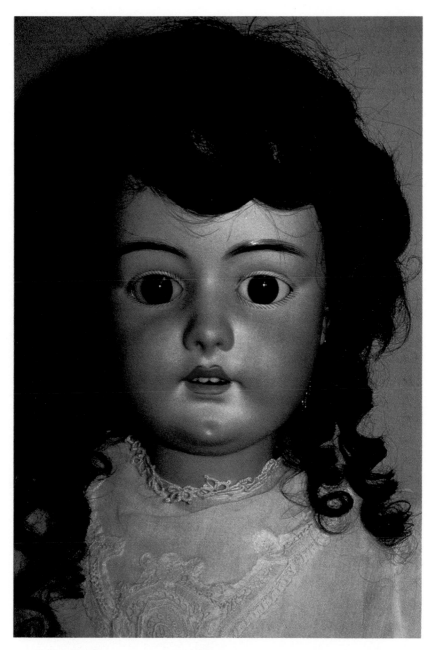

36″ Simon & Halbig mold number 1079 on fully jointed composition body, brown almond-shaped sleep eyes and brown human hair wig. Open mouth and pierced ears. Courtesy Diane Hoffman. $1,200.00

Simon & Halbig

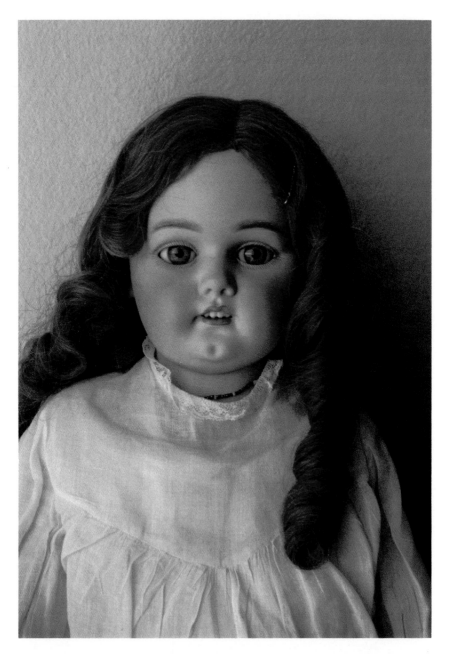

29″ Shoulder head on kid body with bisque lower arms. Pierced ears, human hair wig and open mouth. Marks: Germany/Simon & Halbig/1080 S & H 13. Courtesy Sally Freeman. $995.00

31″ Marked: S & H Santa 1249. Open mouth, sleep eyes and molded eyebrows. On fully jointed composition body. Made by Simon & Halbig. Courtesy Kimport Dolls. $1,300.00

Simon & Halbig

From left around in circle: 18″ Heinrich Handwerck/Simon & Halbig/1. Open mouth, sleep eyes with lashes. In blue: marked S&H 1249/DEP/Germany/Santa/6½. Molded brows, sleep eyes, open mouth with dark ''v'' in center of lower lip. Front: marked 320-8/DEP and 17″ tall. Open mouth and sleep eyes. Jointed body that swivels at waist. Maker unknown, but very unusual body. In green: marked DRGM 201013./A.2/OM. 17″ tall and has voice box in head that is operated by a lever. Bisque shoulder head on bisque shoulder plate. In yellow: marked 1894/AM 5 DEP/Made in Germany. Socket head on jointed body, open mouth and 18″ tall. Nearest pole in back: 18″ marked Armand Marseille/Germany/390/A.2.M. Open mouth with sleep eyes and lashes, jointed body. Courtesy Reins Collection. 18″ - $395.00. 17″, #1249 - $625.00. 17″, A.M. Cryer in Head - $425.00. 18″, #1894 - $400.00

13″ Simon & Halbig "Flapper" with adult composition body. Marks: S & H, on bisque head. Courtesy Kimport Dolls. $1,250.00

10″ All original bisque head with cloth body and nicely detailed bisque lower arms and hands. Bisque legs with painted-on white socks and black high-heeled boots. Marks: S & H. Courtesy Barbara Earnshaw. $900.00

15″ Marked: 1448/Simon & Halbig/S & H. Closed mouth character child with glass eyes and sweet expression. She is on a fully jointed composition body. Courtesy Pauly Deem. $1,800.00

17″ marked: S & H/DEP/1279/Germany/7½″.Socket head with sleep eyes, open mouth with two teeth and has accented lips with impressed center dot on lower lip. Dimples and on jointed body. Courtesy Reins Collection. $995.00

Simon & Halbig

Left to right: Marked: 1299/Simon & Halbig/3½. Doll is 10″ doll has open mouth with two upper teeth. Center doll is 19″ with open mouth and marked: S & H 1079/DEP/Germany/8. Next is the baby marked: C Made in Germany 7/237/JDK/Hilda and is 12″ tall. Has open mouth with two teeth and wobble tongue. Courtesy Reins Collection. 10″ - $350.00. 19″ - $750.00. 12″ Hilda - $1,700.00.

14″ Simon & Halbig with bisque shoulder head, open mouth with six teeth, set eyes. Straw stuffed muslin body with cardboard inset to house bellows voice box. Pull string on left side of body and doll cries ''mama''. Original costume. Courtesy Penny Pendlebury. $385.00

STOBEL & WILKINS

Stobel & Wilkins imported, produced and distributed dolls from New York City and Cincinnati, Ohio from 1864 into the 1930's. They used many different German doll head/body makers to make their bisque-headed dolls. Sample marks:

CHILD DOLL: Open mouth, glass eyes:
8″ - $125.00	20″ - $395.00
12″ - $200.00	24″ - $475.00
16″ - $300.00	

8¾″ All original Scotch boy marked: 200 12/0 Germany. Made by Stobel & Wilkins. Mohair wig, set blue eyes, open mouth with four teeth and on crude five-piece papier mache body with painted boots with heels. 10″ Girl, all original and incised: Halbig K star R 26 M: On good quality five-piece body, mohair wig, sleep eyes and mouth with four teeth. Courtesy Florence Maine. 8¾″ - $150.00

TINTED BISQUE

Tinted bisque dolls differ from the unglazed porcelain parian dolls in that the bisque has color in it. The "skin tones" are not white as they are in the parian-type dolls. Most were made in Germany.

16½" Blue scarf tinted bisque with blue painted eyes. Said to represent Empress Louise of Prussia as she is depicted in a painting descending the stairs at Schonbrunn Palace on her way to Napoleon to plead for her people. The painting is by Gustav Richter. Courtesy Kitty Best. $800.00

4″ Tall head of tinted bisque with applied bows in molded hairdo. Deep ruffle applied on shoulder plate and ears are pierced. Has masses of little curls at forehead. Painted features. Courtesy Diane Hoffman. Head only - $200.00

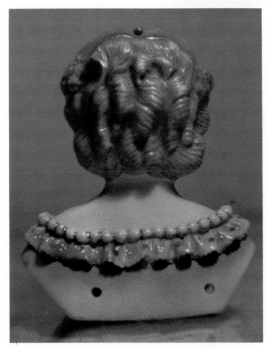

Back of tinted bisque hairdo with drop curls at different levels, and comb marks throughout hairdo. Courtesy Diane Hoffman.

Tinted Bisque

19½" Tinted bisque with blue ribbon molded in blonde bobbed hair, pierced ears and painted blue eyes. Three sew holes, cloth body with leather arms with hands that have separately stitched fingers. Courtesy Kitty Best. $800.00

14" Glass-eyed tinted bisque with molded hair, marked: Germany//211, followed by a K inside a bell, which is the mark of the Kling firm. Full closed mouth with dark line painted between lips, partly exposed ears and child's hair style. Painted lashes above and below the glass eyes. Courtesy Kitty Best. $625.00

UNKNOWN

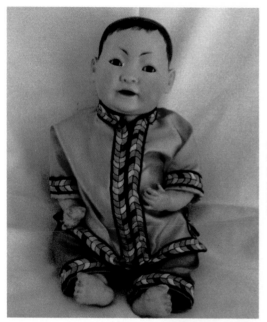

15″ Unmarked bisque head Oriental with open mouth and set eyes. On five-piece baby body, with right arm and hand molded in a bent position. Painted black hair. Courtesy Sally Freeman. $1,500.00

16″ Closed mouth, turned head. Has one-piece shoulder and head, set eyes and is incised "7" on back of head and on lower part of shoulder plate. Is on gussetted kid body with bisque lower arms. Courtesy Florence Maine. $995.00

Unknown

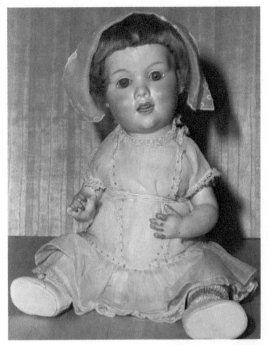

13″ Baby on five-piece bent leg baby body. Bisque head is marked: 410 3. Maker is unknown. Sleep blue eyes, open mouth with two rows of teeth. The lower teeth RETRACT when doll is placed on its back, and teeth are replaced by molded tongue. May have been made by Armand Marseille. Courtesy Bess Fantl. $750.00

23″ Bisque head marked: B/6. Open/closed mouth with molded and painted upper teeth, has very protruding ears and glass sleep eyes. A very smiling character. On fully jointed composition body. (Author). $2,200.00

14″ Beautiful German lady doll dressed in original clothes. Bisque head with glass eyes and closed mouth. Bisque lower arms with rest being cloth stuffed. Maker unknown, but may have been Simon and Halbig. (Author). $895.00

21″ Incised 165/10, on jointed toddler body, pale blue eyes and has watermelon style closed mouth. Some collectors call them Kestners, but maker is uncertain. Courtesy Marlowe Cooper. $7,200.00

Unknown

16" Rare German character doll that is only marked: 6/Germany. Wide open/closed mouth with tongue that is molded, very blue set eyes, original blonde wig and pate and original white cotton dress. Ball-jointed composition body. Courtesy Elizabeth Burke. $2,200.00

18" Belton-type German Fashion Lady with bisque socket head on bisque shoulder plate. Closed mouth and paperweight eyes. Marks: 51/8, on head. Courtesy Kimport Dolls. $1,300.00

15½" Bisque shoulder head with fully closed mouth and dark line painted between lips. Decal style eyebrows, paperweight eyes and on kid body with bisque lower arms. Courtesy Kimport Dolls. $995.00

8½" Oriental bisque head on five- piece composition body. Ca. 1910. Open mouth and glass eyes. Marks: 7/0. Courtesy Kimport Dolls. $495.00

Unknown

9″ Bisque head marked: 39-17. Closed mouth and dressed in all original Rough Rider outfit. Glass eyes, painted-on black shoes. Courtesy Kimport Dolls. $395.00

10½″ Oriental baby on bent limb baby body. Incised: Germany J, on back of head and has: 7 A 2 R out of sight on lower neck socket. Head is 9″ in circumference, rather dark in color and is a heavy material, such as composition or painted over pottery. Black hair appears sprayed-on as the head is smooth with no mold lines. Courtesy Florence Maine. $495.00

13½" Tall with 7" head circumference. Excellent quality bisque with painted intaglio eyes, open/closed mouth with two teeth. Long pointed chin, rather jutting jaw and has elongated ears. Long slender lady body jointed only at the shoulders and hips. Marks: 185/20/F.B./616. Courtesy Elizabeth Burke. $1,500.00

13" "Roman Peasant Boy" Marks: $\mathcal{M}$ /4/0. Maker unknown. Brown set eyes, open mouth with five teeth. Original costume, black mohair wig and on fully jointed composition body, straight wrists. Courtesy Bess Fantl. $350.00

Unknown

7¾″ Tall with 5″ head circumference. Bisque head is marked: Made in Germany// 19/0//DEP. Original paperweight blue eyes, old clothes, open mouth with teeth and on five-piece crude papier mache body. Courtesy Elizabeth Burke. $195.00

8″ Bisque head marked: 1910/Germany/W/12/0. Glass eyes, open mouth, painted shoes and all original. Courtesy Kimport Dolls. $175.00

18″ Unmarked turned shoulder plate head of bisque that is excellent quality. Kid body with bisque lower arms. Closed mouth. Courtesy Kimport Dolls. $1,100.00

4¾" Cloth body with bisque shoulder plate, painted features and is marked: 7 (or I) 02 12/0, on back of shoulder plate. Bisque arms and legs, and painted on brown shoes. Original suit. Molded, painted hair. Courtesy Rosalind Cranor. $145.00

7½" Unmarked fur-covered doll on good quality five-piece papier mache body. Feet and hands are not well defined, but hands resemble paws, while feet look human. Set blue eyes and closed mouth. Fur is loose enough to determine she has a solid dome head. Has ears that do not stand up any longer. Courtesy Florence Maine. $185.00

Unknown

4¾" Tall with bisque shoulder plate on cloth body. Back of shoulder plate is marked: 693 13/0. Molded side part hair with bun in back, bisque arms and legs. Painted features. Original clothes including slip with original pantaloons underneath. Courtesy Rosalind Cranor. $225.00

11½" Painted eye German Fashion with shoulder head and lower arms of bisque. Remainder of body is kid. May be original clothes and wig. Courtesy Barbara Earnshaw. $495.00

INDEX

MOLD NUMBERS

Two Important Tools For The
Astute Antique Dealer, Collector and Investor

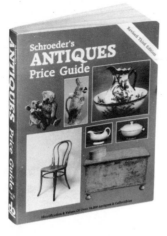

Schroeder's Antiques Price Guide

The very best low cost investment that you can make if you are really serious about antiques and collectibles is a good identification and price guide. We publish and highly recommend **Schroeder's Antiques Price Guide.** Our editors and writers are very careful to seek out and report accurate values each year. We do not simply change the values of the items each year but start anew to bring you an entirely new edition. If there are repeats, they are by chance and not by choice. Each huge edition (it weighs 3 pounds!) has over 56,000 descriptions and current values on 608 - 8½x11 pages. There are hundreds and hundreds of categories and even more illustrations. Each topic is introduced by an interesting discussion that is an education in itself. Again, no dealer, collector or investor can afford not to own this book. It is available from your favorite bookseller or antiques dealer at the low price of $9.95. If you are unable to find this price guide in your area, it's available from Collector Books, P. O. Box 3009, Paducah, KY 42001 at $9.95 plus $1.00 for postage and handling.

Schroeder's INSIDER and Price Update

A monthly newsletter published for the antiques and collectibles marketplace.

The **"INSIDER"**, as our subscribers have fondly dubbed it, is a monthly newsletter published for the antiques and collectibles marketplace. It gives the readers timely information as to trends, price changes, new finds, and market moves both upward and downward. Our writers are made up of a panel of well-known experts in the fields of Glass, Pottery, Dolls, Furniture, Jewelry, Country, Primitives, Oriental and a host of other fields in our huge industry. Our subscribers have that "inside edge" that makes them more profitable. Each month we explore 8-10 subjects that are "in", and close each discussion with a random sampling of current values that are recorded at press time. Thousands of subscribers eagerly await each monthly issue of this timely 16-page newsletter. A sample copy is available for $3.00 postpaid. Subscriptions are postpaid at $24.00 for 12-months; 24 months for $45.00; 36 months for $65.00. A sturdy 3-ring binder to store your **Insider** is available for $5.00 postpaid. This newsletter contains NO paid advertising and is not available on your newsstand. It may be ordered by sending your check or money order to Collector Books, P. O. Box 3009, Paducah, KY 42001.